THE
RIGHT
WAY TO
KEEP
Ponies

In the same series
Solving Horse and Pony Problems

THE
RIGHT
WAY TO
KEEP
Ponies

Words of Wisdom
from An Experienced
Veterinarian

Hugh Venables

Illustrated by
Christine Bousfield

THE LYONS PRESS
GUILFORD, CONNECTICUT

An imprint of The Globe Pequot Press

The Lyons Press is an imprint of The Globe Pequot Press.

10 9 8 7 6 5 4 3 2 1

Printed in the Unites States of America

Library of Congress Cataloging-in-Publication Data

Venables, Hugh.
    The right way to keep ponies : words of wisdom from an experienced
veterinarian / Hugh Venables ; illustrated by Christine Bousfield.—
1st ed.
        p. cm.
    ISBN 1-59228-007-2 (trade cloth)
    1. Ponies.   I. Title.
SF285.3.V46 2004
636.1'63—dc22

                                    2004000640

Contents

Introduction vii
1. A Pony in the Family 1
2. Where to Keep a Pony? 9
3. The Pony's Field. 17
4. Housing for a Pony 27
5. Floors and the Pony's Bed. 35
6. Equipping the Stable 45
7. Grass as Pony Food 55
8. Extra Food 65
9. Grooming Your Pony 75
10. Clipping and Clothing 89
11. The Pony's Tack 103
12. Outings for Your Pony 119
13. Veterinary Care. 129
14. The Feet and Legs 149
15. Buying a Pony. 165
    Glossary 179
    Index. 185

Introduction

At least half, and probably more, of the fun of having ponies comes from looking after them. Today's pony becomes as much a part of the family as any well-loved dog or cat.

The equine animal is not easy to keep in good health. If we wish to ride we must do more than just pay for our mount's housing, feeding, and clothing. We have to be prepared to feed it, groom it ourselves, and to clean the stable; perhaps also to train it, as well as looking after its general health and welfare.

The number of ponies kept for pleasure is steadily increasing. Many of the people who buy one have had no previous experience of looking after such a large animal, and will have no one nearby to whom they can turn for reliable advice. You might laugh at hearing of a man who tried to feed his horse on meat and dog food. Nevertheless, it is all too easy for the novice to make assumptions which the experienced ponykeeper finds astonishing, simply because the novice does not appreciate how different the pony is from other animals he has dealt with.

A pony is very similar to a horse. For most practical purposes it can be considered as a horse, but in a smaller, hardier version. Care of the pony is the prime concern of this book, because most people's first equine experience is usually with a pony, either their own or their children's. With only slight modification to allow for the greater size and, perhaps in some instances, more aristocratic breeding, all that is said about the care of the pony can be applied to the care of the horse.

Much that is written and said about the care of ponies is arguable; some is downright wrong. Experts vary widely in their opinions on any one aspect though, as experience grows, you realize that one particular routine or method may be no better or worse than another.

The suggestions given in this book are the product of one person's accumulated knowledge and practical experience. As far as possible, reasons for each point have been given. I hope this will help you to remember the right way rather than the wrong, and save you from being burdened by traditional—and sometimes erroneous—dogma.

Chapter One

A PONY IN THE FAMILY

Whether or not to buy a pony is the big question. The young rider looks forward eagerly to many happy hours caring for a pony; grooming, training, and riding. Parents, however, often anticipate a pony's arrival with less enthusiasm, bearing in mind the cost of keeping it, and of providing the equipment that is needed. For some, too, there is the unpleasant feeling that they know little or nothing about the day-to-day requirements of such a large animal with the added worry of not being able to cope with problems such as illness.

The addition of a pony to the family brings many benefits. Parents find relief from months, perhaps years, of nagging and begging by their horse-crazy children. They can feel with confidence that other owners of ponies will encourage their offspring to enjoy stimulating and healthy recreation, involving plenty of exercise in the open air. A child's sense of responsibility and a degree of self-control are both developed by caring for a living animal. So too is the ability to accept disappointment, such as when tragedy strikes and the pony goes lame the day before an important event.

Riding in the country brings the opportunity to watch and learn about agriculture, the way plants and trees grow, and the behavior of wild animals; all much more interesting when seen at first hand—and from the back of one's mount—than when viewed on television. This, and the pleasure of just being with the pony, make ponykeeping a worthwhile occupation for any young person—and for those who are not so young, too.

Fig. 1. Riding in the country.

Riders of ponies also have much to gain socially, meeting other enthusiasts at local pony hunts, shows and trail rides. Their parents are likely to become involved as well, and many enjoy attending pony-oriented gatherings in a supporting role. Most pony events are held in pleasant places; the people are friendly and the social life comes to involve the whole family, not just its riding members. Unfortunately, parents can sometimes become too competitive, and the pleasant atmosphere may be lost as winning becomes all important, although this becomes a concern only relatively rarely.

Buying a Pony
Despite strong arguments in favor of acquiring a pony, there are some circumstances under which it is better not to buy one. Getting a pony as a status symbol is foolish because it differs from most other indicators of wealth in being a living creature and requiring constant and critical attention. A pony cannot be ridden occasionally and just turned out in the field when not

wanted, in the same way as a toy is returned to its storage box. Under such treatment the animal is likely to become difficult to manage and unreliable. Whether it is being worked or not, a pony still needs daily feeding and watering, shelter in bad weather, proper attention to the feet, and so on. Neglect of these basics is cruel to the animal, and is particularly likely when a pony is bought for a child who does not really want one.

Assuming that someone is truly enthusiastic about having a pony, is their riding good enough and their knowledge of horses sufficient to be able to deal with the care of one yet? Though many children long for a pony from a very early age, it is probably unwise to buy one in most cases until the age of about eight or nine years old. If younger than this, the child is unlikely to be strong enough, or a sufficiently competent rider, to go far off of the leading rein, nor will the child be able to make much of a contribution to looking after the animal.

There is a general tendency to overestimate one's own, and one's children's, capabilities—and this goes for riding as much as anything else. One has to be *taught* to ride properly. Adequate lessons at a good, reputable riding school are essential before a pony is purchased. The rider must master the elements of equitation and how too cope with the pony *before* it arrives. Hours spent hanging around riding schools and other people's ponies (without being a nuisance, of course) are not entirely wasted, as some of the "do's and don'ts" of handling horses can be learned by such exposure. But so long as there is any doubt about the young rider's confidence and abilities, it is best to delay acquiring a pony rather than risk the rider being hurt or frightened.

The cost of purchasing a pony and its maintenance should be estimated in advance, as it is, unfortunately, expensive to keep a pony. Even a tough, hardy pony with only the most basic, secondhand equipment, is not cheap to maintain, although it will be relatively inexpensive to buy. Actually, the purchase price of a pony is usually the least of the problems. Besides providing a field and shelter and food, other expenses crop up: shoeing, for example, and repairs to saddlery; attention to the field and its fences to keep them in reasonable order; also, can you afford the cost of veterinary treatment for regular care, or if the pony becomes seriously ill?

It is sometimes said that time is money, but both are needed when you have a pony. Some supervision is required if young people are to ride safely. They must wear hard hats (preferably meeting American Society for Testing and Materials, or ASTM, specifications) with the chin strap always fastened. When people go riding it is a good idea to know roughly where they are going, and approximately when they intend to be back. If the pony's owner is away, another member of the family may have to step in and look after the animal; on a cold, dark, winter evening this requires some dedication. The invasion of the house by all the accoutrements of ponykeeping also demands remarkable tolerance from other members of the family who are not necessarily very enthusiastic about equine matters.

The Mind of the Pony

Ponies differ from most other domestic pets in size, and especially in temperament. With experience, handling horses or ponies becomes very easy, and the knowledgeable horseman almost seems to read his animals' minds. This understanding grows from thoughtful observation, watching what they do and learning why they do it, so that the best horsemen come to anticipate a horse's reactions in a given circumstance.

It is helpful to have a wider understanding of the background of the equine species. Wild ponies lived on open grassland; their cousins, the zebras for example, still do in parts of Africa. On these plains they move about in herds, grazing and wandering perhaps ten miles a day, perhaps twenty, just looking for their natural food, which is grass. Wild ponies are on the move, slowly, for much of the time.

Predatory beasts on the great plains depended upon catching these ancestral ponies for food; zebras today still have to keep a wary eye open all the time for carnivores, such as lions. Herbivorous animals instinctively stay together, as twenty eyes are better than two. Ponies today still have this herd instinct. The eyesight of ponies is well developed, particularly for spotting something moving—it could be a lion—a long way off. Ponies' eyes are placed in the sides of their heads. (See fig. 2.)

Ponies tend to be nervous and jumpy. Their wild ancestors had to be alert all the time to spot enemies, and relied for survival on fast reactions and the ability to flee. The modern pony still has the same automatic reaction to danger, by running away. If confined and unable to gallop, the pony becomes terrified, sometimes struggling wildly and quite irrationally, often making things worse. A really frightened pony becomes difficult to manage and often behaves in an unpredictable manner, as instinct takes over from training. One of the secrets of success in handling ponies lies in anticipating the causes of fear, so that the animal can be kept out of the way of potentially frightening circumstances or distracted from them.

All horses and ponies have a very acute sense of hearing. Those mobile ears tell the animal from which direction even small sounds are coming. Make use of this when walking up to the pony. If you talk, then the pony knows where you are, and you don't just appear unexpectedly. This gives the pony greater confidence in you, particularly when your voice is familiar. When out riding, notice how the pony flicks an ear back to listen when you speak. After a while, most ponies can be taught to respond to a few verbal commands: "walk," "trot," "stand," and so

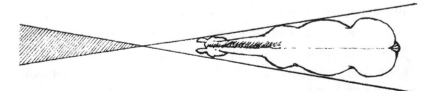

Fig. 2. A pony can see almost all around its body without moving its head. The shaded area is the field of binocular vision. (i.e. this area can be seen with both eyes at once).

on. These must always be the same words, and, very importantly, said in the same tone of voice. Don't forget that a pony is sensitive to, and will be upset by, strange sounds; these include loud talking or shouting, which never serve any useful purpose with ponies, and can do a lot of harm.

Alertness, acute hearing, and good eyesight are features of ponies, but why else do they sometimes behave apparently quite unpredictably? The pony differs from humans and, to some extent, from animals like dogs, in having a very good memory, but little logical thought. All training is therefore achieved by the same system of responses to a particular command, followed by a reward. As you ride, you do this by applying an "aid," or instruction, in the form of, for example, pressure on the left rein for a left turn. When the pony responds, and turns, you release the pressure, and this is the reward. The pony does not like the feel of the bit being pulled, even if very gently, against the side of the mouth. From past experience, the pony knows that it is to turn, and then the uncomfortable feeling will stop. Of course, it would be just as easy to throw the rider, and gallop off into the distance. Fortunately ponies are not usually intelligent enough to work that out, nor do they realize their own strength; such behavior is usually not in their nature.

Always be absolutely consistent with the pony. Even the simplest matter, like leading in a halter is really further training. If the animal is allowed to misbehave—pausing to eat grass for instance—it gets the idea that this is all right. Such faulty behavior should be corrected immediately, often just with a sharp word. The pony that stops to eat grass should be made to walk on, and will soon come to realize that this is not allowed.

In correcting a pony, firmness, but not brutality, is needed. There is no point in trying to hurt or frighten the animal. This only makes a pony nervous and difficult to handle; it will remember the whole incident as a nasty experience, but will not know why. Determination on your part is important though, and generally it is you who should decide what the pony is to do, and get him to do it. However, this should not involve a huge battle, and if occasionally you find that you have asked too much, then it is better to give in a little than to try to fight it out. Absolute confidence is essential in riding and handling ponies; they have an astonishing ability to sense human nervousness and exploit it.

Approaching the Pony

A few words of greeting to the pony are helpful at any time, and will ensure that a resting animal is not frightened by your wandering up unnoticed. Always approach from the front, because otherwise the pony could kick out with its hind legs. Approach slowly and quietly; if you bound up shouting and laughing, the pony may begin to wonder what on earth this thing is, and with good reason!

Ponies' skins are highly sensitive, and they find very light handling ticklish, so always stroke or pat gently, but firmly. Most ponies and horses, once they have had a look at you, seem to enjoy a pat on the neck, though they often dislike being patted

Fig. 3. Always offer a tidbit with your hand held flat.

on the face, and can you really blame them? Handling the head has to be done with some care, moving slowly and deliberately so that you don't startle the pony, and being particularly careful about touching the ears. Some animals resent this very much.

Ponies differ from other animals that might be kept as pets, such as dogs and cats. They sometimes don't seem to enjoy being stroked for its own sake; rather they tolerate it in the hope that a tidbit might appear. Favorite treats include carrots, strong peppermints, and crackers or cookies. The carrots should be cut lengthwise into thick pieces, because if they are sliced into round slivers, there is a chance that a greedy pony could swallow one whole and choke on it. Apples are also enjoyed by ponies, in a rather dribbly way. These, too, should be cut into longer pieces.

Horses and ponies are traditionally offered lumps of sugar, but I do not recommend this. The reason is not that sugar damages a pony's teeth (which is unlikely, unless you give it by the fifty-pound bag) but because ponies are often too fond of it, and seem to become almost addicted. The result is a pony that can become very naughty, nipping and even kicking in its eagerness for yet another lump. Too much of any treat can spoil a pony, of course, but none as fast as sugar.

When you give a tidbit, always offer a small amount with your hand held flat, so that the pony can pick up the delicacy without taking your fingers as well. When giving treats, try to avoid the development of naughty tricks like nipping, and never encourage this by letting the pony search your pockets for bits. The best behavior results from treats coming only on well-defined occasions. When you go to catch the pony in the field, and when it is turned out again, are good times to give a delicacy, and this will make catching the animal easier. An occasional treat if the pony does particularly well in training, for example, is also a useful way of indicating your pleasure. But if you want to give your pony a special treat, it is better to make up a really delicious feed than to give a lot of snacks by hand.

Chapter Two

WHERE TO KEEP A PONY?

Before you buy, here is the first problem you must face: Where are you going to keep the pony?

In summer there may be little difficulty, as almost any animal can live outside, day and night, at this time of year. Winter is another matter.

Whatever the time of year, don't forget that a pony, being a large animal, eats a considerable quantity of food every day. This applies whether it consists of grazing, living on hay and concentrates (grain-based feed), or a combination of both. A half-acre paddock, for example, will not be able to provide enough grass for even one pony throughout the year. In addition, those hard hooves, whether shod or not, can cut up such a small area very badly. You may find the "grazing" is soon turning into a swamp, with the dejected animal standing in the middle of it, fetlock-deep in mud.

If you have only a small area in which to keep the pony, then you may be able to rent or lease extra grazing land not too far from home, or board the pony in another pony owner's pasture. Alternatively, wear and tear on your field can be reduced by keeping the pony in a stable for part of the time. This will mean you will need to feed extra hay and grain, the amount depending on the pony's size, the amount of work it is doing, and how much grass is available in the paddock.

One and a half to two acres of reasonable quality grazing is the minimum required for a pony that is to live outdoors on a diet based on grass. It is frequently asserted that a pony can live outside all year, requiring no shelter from cold winds, rain, or the snow in winter, nor from flies in the summer. And it is certainly true that hardier ponies can survive some very tough winters with no shelter at all. But the important word is *survive*, not thrive, and these ponies are probably not expected to work, even on weekends. More important, they have very large areas of land over which to roam in search of food and where they have a better chance of finding some shelter behind rocks or trees. This is very different from the unfortunate animal enclosed in a small, bare paddock. It is very likely that the life of a pony will be shortened by needing to survive if kept outdoors and left to deal with the rigors of winter. Even more supplementary feeding will be needed for the pony that is kept out all the time, without any shelter.

So, though you may plan that your pony should, basically, lead an outdoor life—and most ponies are best kept in this manner— you should acknowledge the need for some sort of simple building. It may only be the most basic shelter, made with walls of straw bales or plastic sheeting, and a roof of corrugated metal, but it must provide somewhere to get out of the wind and allow the coat to dry. The shelter should also have a hard floor to enable the animal to stand on a dry surface. Preferably it should be bedded down to provide a resting place for at least a few hours each day.

Fig. 4. The unfortunate pony in a small, bare paddock.

Contrary to popular belief, horses and ponies *do* lie down if they have somewhere reasonably comfortable to do so. Would you settle down for a nap in four inches of freezing mud? On milder days in early spring, it is obvious how much ponies appreciate a chance to rest, for they will often lie stretched out, almost as if dead, in the warm sunshine.

Most ponies are in the habit of lying down for a few hours during the night or early morning in summer, although you may not see them. Of course, equines can also doze standing up, and many get much of their sleep in that way. In winter, outdoor ponies will seldom lie down and rest at night, partly because there is nowhere warm and dry to lie down, and partly because at night it may be so cold that they have to walk around just to keep warm. For this reason, any lying down is done during the warmest part of the day, around lunchtime, when you are around. You may gain the false impression that the pony lies down to sleep more in winter than in summer.

Keeping a Pony on Grass

The easiest method of keeping a pony, and the most economical in terms of labor and cost, is in a paddock with a shelter or stable into which the animal can go at will. Under this system, less work falls on the keeper, who only has to go and look the pony over once a day, check the water, provide the food, and keep the shelter bedded down, cleaning it out from time to time.

If left loose in a field, the pony will not require daily exercise such as would be necessary if it were confined to a stable; wandering about keeps the animal moderately fit and prevents an unpleasant excess of energy when it is time to be ridden. Freedom to graze or rest is a more natural life than that of the stabled animal, and ponies kept in this way are generally more healthy. Some individuals are not really hardy enough to live out, however, and need to be more carefully looked after and stabled at night during inclement weather.

Fig. 5. A shaggy coat can get very muddy when the pony rolls.

There are problems with keeping a pony outdoors all the time. One is that the animal may be wet and dirty when you want to ride. In winter, particularly, the shaggy coat gets very muddy when the pony rolls, and it is very hard to get it clean. Outdoor ponies never look really clean at this time of year. A pony kept out on pasture can become remarkably fit in summer with plenty of exercise. In winter, however, the heavy winter coat causes excessive sweating, so that little fast work can be done. On the other hand there may be some savings in cost and maintenance, as no blankets may be required. Furthermore, being free to graze all the time (as long as there is something in the field) the pony requires somewhat less supplementary feed in winter, although some will always be needed.

The Half-and-Half Turnout System
A modification of the method described above, the half-and-half turnout system involves stabling the pony by day in summer, but

by night in winter. The rest of the time is spent turned out in the field. This follows the animal's natural inclinations, since in summer most ponies prefer to be inside during the day, where they can get relief from annoying flies, and in winter they shelter at night when it is the coldest.

This system also gives the rider the best of both worlds in summer, for the pony is in and ready to ride during the day; at night both sustenance and outdoor exercise are taken! Stabling for part of the time during the summer also allows you to restrict the amount of lush grass that is eaten, an important matter with ponies, otherwise they can easily become too heavy. This system is not quite as convenient in winter, with the pony being out by day and stabled at night. The animal is not always standing ready to be ridden. This is not very important, because riders are usually occupied with school or work for most of the daylight hours in winter. In fact, this system of ponykeeping can suit most people quite well, since the animal requires attention only first thing in the morning, and then again in the evening.

Of course, there is a bit more work involved in keeping a pony this way, compared with being out at pasture. The animal has to be turned out and brought in, the stable requires daily cleaning and bedding down, the water bucket needs replenishing, and in winter at least two feedings a day will be required. Also, because more time is spent in it, the stabling itself has to be better built. It must be equipped with a door, and a window for ventilation, rather than relying on a wide entrance (perhaps closed with a rail) as a field shelter does, and a solid roof to keep the pony and its bedding dry and warm at all times.

If kept in at night in winter, the pony can be partially clipped, and removal of that heavy coat will make the work go faster. It will also necessitate the wearing of blankets to keep warm: a waterproof New Zealand rug is best when outside, and a quilted or similar insulated stable blanket when inside. Checking and changing the blankets, as well as their care, also adds to the work of keeping the pony. Although out for only a relatively small proportion of the time, the pony will require almost as much hay and concentrates as the animal that is stabled all the time, but there is less need for exercise and grooming.

The Stabled Pony

A pony may be kept in a large box stall day and night, but will still require considerable attention to be kept fit and occupied. On the other hand, such a pony is ready to be ridden at virtually any time, and is able to do hard, fast work. An animal as fit as this may become too full of energy at times, and requires a more skilled rider.

A stabled pony requires about two hours' exercise each day. This movement is essential for the animal's health, as it stimulates digestion, improves circulation, and aids in removal of waste gases from the body. Especially important is that it improves blood flow to the feet and limbs. Daily work also keeps the pony fit and prevents boredom. Regular grooming is required, as is feeding three or four times a day, and the stable will require frequent attention. All of this may be too much to be easily arranged around school, or some other full-time occupation.

Considerable skill and experience are required to keep a stabled pony in good condition, so that it is fit but not unmanageable. The stabled life is quite unnatural and the diet entirely artificial. Even if you do all the work yourself, it is more expensive to keep a pony indoors all the time in terms of feed and bedding, shoeing, and equipment like blankets. Well-designed stabling with an adequate storage area is particularly important when so much work is done there.

The Decision

Of the three systems described, the most popular, and probably the best for small ponies, is one where the animal is turned out all the time, with a shelter that can be used when desired. The pony can then be shut in if necessary, on the night before a show or a hunt, for example, and can be enclosed in summer if excessive amounts of grass are being eaten. For young riders, the grass-fed only method has the distinct advantage that any spare energy is expended in grazing rather than in mischief, as it might be if the food came only in a bucket, and hay net. From the point of view of the parents, a pony that is on pasture requires minimum attention, and the hardy type is usually self-sufficient most of the time.

For a larger pony, or one that may be expected to be ridden hard during the winter, the half-and-half system allows reasonable fitness to be maintained, without any build-up of excess energy. It is also a suitable method for keeping a less hardy animal. Stabling ponies all the time—and horses as well, for that matter—should be avoided, unless they are to be worked very hard, as they can become difficult to handle. This happens more often than people may realize. The result is that much of the pleasure of owning a pony can be lost, since the rider may not always be sure that he is the one in control of the animal.

Chapter Three

THE PONY'S FIELD

Wandering around the field foraging for food will help to keep a pony healthy. This is much closer to the natural way of life than standing cooped up in a stable all day, waiting for food to be brought. However, keeping your pony in a field first requires that you have, or you can find, a suitable pony-proof field.

If you or your family have a sizeable paddock of your own, the problem is not that great. Do not overestimate the ability of a small piece of ground to support one or more ponies. Between one-and-a-half and two acres of grazing per pony is needed at the minimum. On less than this, do not be surprised when all the edible grass soon disappears, and the animals require considerable quantities of other food, both hay and concentrates, to be provided for them throughout the year. It is also easy to underestimate how much *damage* horses or ponies can do to grassland. Their feet wear large bare and muddy patches around troughs, feeding areas, shelter entrances, gateways, and other favorite standing places.

If you have only a small paddock of your own, you may need to rest it every few months to let the grass recover, while the pony is grazed somewhere else. Rented grazing or boarding may be some distance away, and it can also be costly, if you have to arrange for your pony to be housed elsewhere for any period of time.

Fencing
This is especially a problem with rented land or boarding locations. Fencing may be inadequate and sometimes you may have to reject a field where the fences are in a very poor condition. If

you are using a paddock on a long-term basis, stout fences and proper repairs are a good investment. They will last better, and you will be able to enjoy the peace of mind that comes from knowing that your pony is securely enclosed.

The ideal type of fencing for horses is wooden post and rail or board fencing, or the modern synthetic substitutes. This may be rather expensive though, and requires considerable maintenance to keep it in good order in the case of wood. It is seldom feasible for the average pony owner.

Fences should be examined frequently for signs of wear and tear—broken or loose boards, or ones that the pony might have chewed badly, protruding nails, and posts that need replacing. Though ponies do not typically barge through fences like cattle do, they will definitely make use of any gaps they can find. They have all day to wander around looking for weak places; and the grass is always *so* much greener on the other side . . .

Dry stone walls, if available and when kept in good repair, can provide adequate fencing for smaller ponies. Rivers and streams should not be depended upon to contain ponies, and may actually tempt them to explore further, unless the obstacles are either quite imposing, or made that way by the presence of another fence on the inward side.

So much for what might be termed permanent fences; we must also consider the type that you can install more easily yourself and that can be easily taken down again. Cheaper alternatives to wooden post and rail include posts interspaced with plain wire, or strung with electric wire, or with rubber or PVC strands, or with wire mesh fencing—preferably of the safer type intended specifically for horses.

These types of fencing must be pulled tight or it can be dangerous. Special tools and some strength may be required. Such fences are best put up by a professional, but may not be beyond the capabilities of the average family handyman. If this type of fencing is not drawn very tight, it can be quite dangerous because ponies can very easily get themselves tangled in it and, once caught, they will struggle, and can injure themselves quite badly.

Even with a properly erected wire fence, the lowest strand should be a minimum of 1 to 1½ feet above the ground. Thick wire is less likely than thin wire to become caught behind the heels of an animal's shoes, as well as being more easily visible. Barbed wire is never recommended for ponies. Nasty injuries can occur when a pony gets its foot caught in loose wire. If a rented field is fenced with barbed wire, it is essential to ensure that it is kept taut at all times.

Before turning a pony into a new field, time spent on checking fences for hazards is never wasted; spare ends of wire should be cut off with wire cutters, or secured out of the way with staples.

Fig. 6. Show the electric fence to the pony when it has been newly installed.

For filling gaps in an emergency, there is a lot to be said for the electric fence, which is readily portable, easy to erect, and is well respected. Most ponies, once they have had one shock from it, only have to hear the tick of the battery unit to make them keep clear of the wire. It has a disadvantage in that it may not be clearly visible, so it is necessary to show the fence to the pony when it has been newly installed. This is particularly important if the electric fence is being used to divide a paddock in half, such as when one part is being rested or has been spread with weedkiller.

Gateways

The ideal way of filling the gateway into a field is with a sturdy gate, preferably one that swings easily, opens wide, looks imposing, and has an appropriate latch—not just a piece of string or twisted wire. Some ponies can be very clever at undoing even proper gate latches, and you may find that as a safety measure an additional fastening of the snap-on type (like a big dog-lead catch), or a toggle and ring, is necessary. Fortunately, ponies cannot undo a padlock and chain, nor can trespassers or vandals.

Slip rails are an alternative that is considerably cheaper than a gate, and they are as effective and almost as convenient. Metal loops are used, with either round or sawn rails passing through them. The rails may be secured, if necessary, by drilling holes through each rail and passing a U-shaped peg through one end (see fig. 7). Wire gateways are dangerous and should not be used for horses.

The stretches of fence in a pony's field that are likely to take the most abuse are those around the gate, where the animals assemble at feeding times, and fences separating them from other horses. Ponies will lean over fences and gates to 'talk' to their friends on the other side, sometimes with unfortunate results, with the fences either giving way or entangling the animals as they paw and stamp.

Fig. 7. Slip-rails are fixed by passing a U-shaped peg through one end.

Fig. 8. Wire gateways are dangerous. The wire tends to go slack, and is liable to cause injury.

Ponies that Get Out

Ponies generally escape for a good reason. One is that, as far as the animal is concerned, the gap is there, so why not make use of it? Things always look better on the outside. Regular checking of all the fences is very important, in particular those fences that would allow ponies to stray out onto roads.

Loose animals are a serious danger to themselves in traffic and can also cause nasty accidents, for which their owner may be liable. Claims arising from such incidents can be very large, and the premiums are relatively small, so that it is really essential to take out some sort of liability insurance if you keep horses or ponies.

Even if you have checked all the fences thoroughly you may find that there are still attempts to escape. You should try to find the reason for this, and ask yourself: Is the pony getting enough to eat, or being driven by hunger to look elsewhere for food? A pony may also get out because of loneliness. Horses are naturally gregarious animals, and some seem to find great discomfort in being alone for long periods. Another pony is the ideal companion, but a donkey, or other "pet," will often have a beneficial effect.

There are a few ponies that seem to delight in getting out for the sake of it, and may even jump back into their own field when they have had enough of the outside world. They seem to see each fence as a challenge to their jumping—or scrambling—abilities, though such animals are rare. This fault has to be accepted because, unless you can find a field with colossal fences, there is little that can be done to prevent them getting out, beyond ensuring that they have equine companions, enough food and water, and sufficient work to use up any spare time and energy.

Other Hazards

Before putting your pony into a field, here are some dangers you should look for apart from those in the fences. Bits of old farm machinery, piles of trash, or the odd broken bottle can all cause serious injury and should be cleared away, or fenced off. If you cannot do this, at least try to make the hazard as safe as possible by removing potential traps and sharp projections.

Ponies are, fortunately, basically sensible. They will usually cope very well with rough ground in the field, unless they are driven over it too fast. Even then, once they know the terrain, they will usually find their way around quite cleverly. If you know that there are large numbers of groundhog or woodchuck holes or other hazards in a new field, it is better to prevent the pony from running around wildly when it is first turned out. This excited galloping is never a good thing, because animals may also blindly charge into fences. This can be discouraged by giving ponies a hard day's work before they go into the strange field, and not too much to eat for about six hours before being turned out. The first thought is then "Food!" The pony will get down to the business of grazing right away, and leave any exploring until after a good meal.

Inter-pony Relationships

All horses and ponies prefer companionship to loneliness. But, paradoxically, they may seem to fight viciously when first being introduced to one another, so owners may be worried about the prospect of turning out strange ponies together. The best approach is to let the animals sort things out between themselves, preferably with plenty of space in which to do it. They seldom injure one another deliberately. Accidents are most likely to occur as a result of a pony not looking where it is going, and running into a fence. Obviously an animal that is known to be vicious (though this is very rare) is better kept separated.

It is a good idea to introduce strangers in a completely new field, where neither has a prior claim to the area. They should be expected to sniff each other, and squeal and gallop around for a while. This is worrisome for the human onlookers, but apparently thoroughly enjoyed by the participants, as is the play-biting and kicking. If you are worried about the risks of kicks, injuries are minimized by having the ponies' hind shoes removed until they have settled down, usually in just a few days.

When ponies live in a group, they usually establish their own special friendships, and particular animals will become the bosses. Care should be taken when extra food is being given, so that there is no bullying of the more submissive individuals (not necessarily the smallest in size) and that each animal gets its fair share; piles of hay, for example, should be set far enough apart so no single pony to be able to monopolize two portions.

Water

Whether your pony is in the field or the stable, a plentiful supply of clean fresh water, available at all times, is essential. In the field a natural spring may be used, provided it is easily accessible and not surrounded by too much mud, and you should check that it does not dry up in hot weather. The same applies if your pony relies on a pond or stream for drinking water.

The automatically filled water trough is convenient, generally reliable, and does not dry up in summer, though it may freeze solid in very cold weather. A glance every once in awhile will ensure that it is full to the correct level, and that the ball valve that shuts off the supply when the trough is full has not stuck, allowing the water to overflow. Not only does this waste water, it also makes the area around the trough very muddy. Because a certain amount of spillage is inevitable from any water trough, and because animals are continually gathering around it, it should be placed on a high, dry part of the field, if possible, and preferably on a concrete or packed dirt pad.

If a concrete or galvanized iron field trough is not available, it may be possible to utilize an old bathtub as a water container. The enameled, full-sized variety will require something more permanent than a simple rubber bath plug to block the drain. A concrete or a wooden plug is best. The undersides of the edges of most baths may be somewhat sharp and a wooden box

Fig. 9. If an old bathtub is used for a water trough, the sides may need to be framed in with wood.

may be needed to prevent the pony's knees from being cut on them (see fig. 9). A cover is also necessary to protect a ball valve or tap from the pony's attentions, to prevent injury and to avoid catching the halter.

A small metal tub or a couple of big buckets can be used to hold the pony's water, but these have the disadvantage that they are easily tipped over. If you are considering carrying your pony's daily water supply, you should estimate a requirement of around 8 gallons per day. Considerably more than this might be needed if hard work is done or if the weather is particularly hot.

The water itself should always be clean (would you like to drink dirty water?), and all troughs require emptying and scrubbing out periodically. A pony should never be left without water, even for a few hours. Not only is it essential for the digestion, and indeed for life, but if a pony is allowed to get very thirsty it will gulp down large quantities of water when it is offered once again, which can cause digestive problems such as colic. To deprive any animal of water is also very unkind. When it is possible to go to the tap and get a drink of water at any time, it is perhaps hard to imagine finding, one day, that it has run dry. But this is how the thirsty animal feels upon going to the water trough and finding it empty.

Chapter Four

HOUSING FOR A PONY

Pony accommodations can range from the smart and expensive stable, complete with tack room and feed storage, a garage for the horse trailer and—of course—the stable cat, to the simplest of field shelters. It doesn't have to be costly and elaborate, however, and adequate stabling can be made by altering a variety of existing buildings. Garden sheds, garages, summer houses, calf pens, barns, and even cart shelters have been used, though some—such as greenhouses—have to be rejected for safety reasons. Alternatively, a building may be put up specially, and here again there are a number of possibilities, depending on financial resources, and the ingenuity of the builder.

Before starting to construct the stable it is best to consider just what is needed. A pony can be housed in either a loose box stall or a straight stall. A box stall provides the freedom to move about at will in what is, effectively, a square or rectangular room. In a straight stall, less popular nowadays for housing horses, the animal is tied by its head to the wall, and there is a passage behind the stall. If you are using a building that was not designed for stabling, it may be easier to provide a straight stall than a box stall, particularly if the place is used only on a temporary basis.

A straight stall is usually about 4 feet wide and, from the front wall, about 10 feet long. There is a passage of some 8 feet behind it. The total floor area is smaller than that of a loose box, which would be from 10 to 12 feet by 10 feet, or just over 100 square feet. The roof height in the stable should be sufficient to ensure that the pony does not bang its head on the ceiling or the roof beams; about 10 feet or more is desirable. If the stable is too low,

Fig. 10. A box stall provides plenty of room for the pony's comfort, plus enough room to move around and lie down. Bedding the stall deeply with clean straw or shavings will keep the pony clean when he rests.

the volume of air is reduced and it may become hot and stuffy. This is unlikely to be a problem where one side of the building is open or closed only with rails, as with many field shelters.

Walls and Roofs

Brick or concrete block walls are probably ideal since they are completely windproof and are good insulators. This is particularly noticeable in summer when concrete stables remain pleasantly cool. These materials are also very long lasting, and stand up against the kicking of most animals. The cost of constructing such a stable may be prohibitive, but a conversion may be feasible.

Perhaps the most popular sort of stabling being built today is the sectional wooden type, which is sturdily constructed. The sections only have to be bolted together on a suitable base to provide almost instant stabling, with very little effort for the purchaser. A number of manufacturers make these buildings and they are a simple, quick, and effective way of housing a pony. Additions can also be made very easily to the original structure, and most of the buildings are designed with this possibility in mind.

With wooden buildings there is a risk that a pony may be able to kick through a thin wall, not only making a hole in the wall but possibly injuring the foot too. Most prefabricated stables are lined with strong boards to above kicking height to prevent this from happening, but if you plan to use some other wooden building, remember this risk. If heavy sawn planks are too costly it may be possible to use cuts of the outermost planks sawn from a tree that still have bark on one side. Though not beautiful these are solid, and usually reasonably cheap.

Building a simple stable or shelter from scratch need not be very difficult. But compare your estimated cost with that of a prefabricated building before you start; it may not be very different. An economical structure can be made using a wood frame with heavy planks nailed to the outside of it. Lined with boards or roofing felt, and with a roof of corrugated iron, this will make a surprisingly good stable. Though it would never be called decorative, if the work is properly done it can look quite neat.

A rough alternative—very temporary but better than nothing in the short term—is to use iron roofing, supported on a wooden frame with walls of straw bales. The bales should be fixed to the frame to ensure that they do not collapse. Since ventilation in such buildings may be minimal they are generally best with only three or three and a half walls, leaving a wide entrance.

Straw bales may also be useful if you are converting another building to provide accommodation for your pony. They can be used to line drafty walls or, with a stout rail, to block a spare doorway. At all times the bales should be strongly secured to prevent them from falling down. They may need to be protected from the pony's attentions (in particular from being eaten) by rails or a gate. Rails, with or without straw bales behind them to protect from drafts, are useful if you want to partition off part of a bigger building to house the pony. They need to be of sufficient height to prevent the pony from jumping them, that is, with a top rail about 4 to 5 feet above the ground, depending on the size of the pony. Middle and lower rails are best spaced between 1 to 1½ feet apart. There is little point in having the bottom bar below about 18 inches from the ground; the pony is unlikely to get under it. If whoever uses the rest of the building would have it kept free of straw, a board 6 inches to 1 foot wide along the ground below the partition should contain the bedding.

When ponies are used to one another, rails may be enough to keep them apart. Generally, however, partitions between animals should be solid, either to the ceiling or effectively so; that is about 6 or 7 feet high. Otherwise, the partition can be boarded for the bottom 4 feet with horizontal or closer vertical rails above. This prevents fighting and kicking because the animals cannot touch each other. In stalls, partitions are usually high enough at the front end to prevent the animals seeing one another, though at the back they are lower, only high enough to prevent kicking.

Tile or slate roofs are a nice addition to stables, but may be prohibitively expensive if you are building a whole stable, and are more common on older barns or converted buildings. These materials are good insulators and, like brick walls, keep a stable noticeably cooler in summer. Sectional stables often have roofs of wood and waterproof felt—effective materials—as are split cedar shingles, which may be used as an attractive alternative on such stabling.

Corrugated iron has the advantage of being cheap. It is easy to manage because it is light, though its sharp edges can inflict nasty injuries and the danger of using it should not be underestimated. It tends to make a building very hot in summer and very cold in winter unless it is lined with wooden boards. Wood also reduces the machine-gun effect of hail on the roof, though most ponies become accustomed to this noise surprisingly quickly.

Doors and Doorways

If there is any choice in the matter it is best if the stable does not face into cold winds, and a south-facing aspect is always preferable. The front of the stable should not be overshadowed, by large trees or other buildings for example, so that its supply of air and light is not reduced.

The doorway should be about 6 to 8 feet high, depending on the size of the pony, which can otherwise get a nasty bump on the head on the top of the door frame. This might create the habit of rushing through the doorway. To avoid banging the pony's hips on the door frame, or the animal squeezing or stepping on the owner when being led out, the doorway should be about 4 feet wide. The door itself should be no bigger than necessary to fill the lower half of the doorway, to a height of about 3 feet 6 inches for an average pony of 13.2 hh. The upper half of the door is not really needed, and it should never be shut unless necessary. The doorway provides important ventilation, as well as allowing the pony to look out and see what is going on. If there are worries that the pony might try to jump the lower door, put in a bar, hinged at one end and fastened with a bolt at the other, or simply passed through metal loops like any other slip rail. This provides a simple, cheap, and effective means of filling the upper half of the doorway, without reducing the ventilation.

The door should open outward and swing open easily, preferably with a hook to fasten it back when the stable is not in use. Since the pony is likely to lean on it, strong hinges are necessary to prevent the door sagging and becoming difficult to open. It needs to be strongly made, too, for many animals have the trick of banging it with a front foot when impatient, especially at feeding time. In doing this a pony would be particularly liable to injury on any sharp edges or projections that might be present on the inside of the door.

Door catches need to be of a type that will stand a lot of wear and tear. They should have no sharp edges which could injure the fingers of the human user, nor any projections which might catch the pony's halter. Bolts are very good, particularly those specially made for stables with a loop and catch arrangement. A snap clip can be put through the loop and this will deter even the most skillful pony from undoing it. A kick catch is also very useful (see fig. 11), especially when you are carrying full buckets of water or nets of hay. Placed low to the ground, this type of catch is also well out of the pony's reach.

The doorway of a pony's field shelter may be considerably bigger than normal door size. Where several animals share a shed it is essential that the entrance should be wide enough to prevent one pony trapping another one inside. It is ideal to have almost the whole of one side (preferably the south side) open. Even if the shelter is only for one pony, there is much to be said for leaving one side completely open as this provides plenty of fresh air without risk of crossdrafts. Ponies are seldom bothered

Fig. 11. Door catches: a stable bolt and a "kick catch."

by cold, though drafts may cause a chill. An outdoor pony, used to outside temperatures, will be quite happy in an open-sided building. Such a shelter can be enclosed with rails across the entrance when you want to keep the pony in.

Windows and Lighting

THE IMPORTANCE OF ADEQUATE VENTILATION CANNOT BE STRESSED ENOUGH. Animals continuously use up the oxygen in the air and breathe out carbon dioxide. This, plus the ammonia produced by decomposing excrement, can make the atmosphere stuffy and unhealthy, unless there is sufficient fresh air entering the building. If ventilation is inadequate, there is also a danger that mold spores from hay or straw may build up to dangerous levels and cause lung damage (COPD see page 140) in ponies that are allergic to them.

Windows are one of the best means of ventilation. The type that is hinged on its lower edge is the best. The sloping pane admits fresh air, which mixes with that in the rest of the stable and produces no draft. Most other types of windows are less suitable but are better than nothing. The window itself should really be above the animal's head. If set lower, it should be barred to prevent the pony from breaking the window and being injured on the broken glass.

There can never be too much daylight in a stable—another reason for having a window in the building, provided the glass is kept clean. It is very helpful to have electric lighting in the stable so that you don't have to attend to the pony at night by light of a flashlight. On the other hand, faulty electrical wiring is one of the commonest causes of fire, so the job of installing the lighting should only be carried out by a qualified electrician.

Light bulbs should be well out of reach of the pony and protected by wire cages to prevent wisps of hay or straw contacting the hot glass. However, the bulbs should not be so far out of reach that it is impossible to change them when they blow, as they all do sometime! Wiring should always be of the heavy duty type, and preferably run through conduit, and, if there is any doubt about the safety of old wiring, it is better replaced or disconnected. Like the rest of the electrical installation, the switches should be where the pony cannot investigate them. The waterproof outdoor models are generally safer and longer-lasting than the ordinary domestic type, though a little more expensive.

Chapter Five

FLOORS AND THE PONY'S BED

Standing on a bare, cold, wet floor all day is not good for anyone. The same goes for ponies. A clean, dry bed of straw protects them from drafts around the legs, provides something soft for the ponies to stand on while they are inside, and helps to keep the stable smelling fresh. A pony also needs to lie down for several hours each day to obtain adequate rest, and a clean straw bed will encourage this. A good bed also prevents injuries, especially to the hocks and elbows, from the floor or walls as the pony lies down, and helps keeps the animal clean.

Fig. 12. A clean straw bed will encourage the pony to lie down.

Bedding is important, too, in keeping the stable floor dry. The hooves of a pony left standing continually in a mixture of manure and urine are likely to exhibit such problems as thrush, a smelly, purulent disease of the frog, which can make a pony very lame.

Flooring

How good a bed you can provide for the pony depends to some extent on the type of floor on which it is to be made. Putting a proper floor in a stable or shelter can sometimes be almost as expensive as putting up the building itself. There are several alternatives as far as flooring is concerned, varying in cost, difficulty of installation, and effectiveness. The floor of the stable should, ideally, be hard, and of a type that is easy to clean and which dries quickly—preferably sloped so that it drains adequately. It should not be so slippery that animals or people have difficulty standing up on it, nor should it be so rough that cleaning becomes impossible.

All this sounds like quite a tall order, but in fact concrete makes a very good and reasonably inexpensive material. Once the earth has been dug out to make room for it, it is fairly easy to lay, particularly if the ready-mixed variety is used. It is best poured over on a layer of rubble or some other hard-core material, and a four-inch depth of concrete is required, with a slope of between one in sixty and one in thirty to help it drain. The drain itself should be placed outside the stable or in a corner rather than in the middle of the floor. If possible, the floor should be a little higher than the surrounding ground, so that no water can seep in from outside.

A screed concrete surface is waterproof and hard, and if leveled with a board while still wet, is not too slippery. Alternatively, grooves can be made in the soft concrete to prevent slipping, though the floor should always be covered with bedding as an additional safeguard. A paving material may be laid over the concrete base.

Compacted clay also makes a very good quality flooring, and is usually quite inexpensive in materials cost and easy enough for the amateur horse owner to install. It provides excellent drainage, and a good, springy cushioned base that is comfortable for the animal to stand and lie on.

Many shelters have no special flooring, and the earth, protected from the rain by the roof and stamped hard by the ponies, often remains surprisingly dry. The success of a bare earth floor depends to some extent on the type of soil in the area, and on the location of the stable. Marshy sites should be avoided.

It also depends on how much time the pony will spend indoors. At the best of times ponies can hardly be said to be house-trained, and it is surprising how much urine and dung one animal can produce in a single night. When trampled on, this can reduce a dry earth floor to a wet, muddy puddle in a very short time. If an earth floor is all that is available, you may find that a deep litter system of bedding down is more successful than one where the stable is completely mucked out on a daily basis.

Types of Bedding Material

Traditionally, straw is considered the ideal bedding material, although other types are quite suitable. Straw should be dry, free from mold and blackness, and of a light golden color, when bought. It should look and smell pleasant. If the straw has only been lightly crushed during harvesting it will not absorb urine so readily and will be more economical, as only a small amount will have to be discarded each day when it becomes soaked through. However, modern methods of harvesting allow for little variation in this. Wheat straw is the best variety, and most readily available except for oat straw.

Barley straw is not considered to be as good as wheat straw because the long barley hairs could irritate the skin of thin-skinned horses. In practice, this is not important for ponies. These mainly lie down inside in winter, when their thick woolly coats give plenty of protection. Oat straw is best avoided, as it is rather sweet tasting and so a pony may eat a considerable quantity of it. This does no serious harm, but straw is bulky and has relatively little nutritional value, so the pony fills up quickly and has nothing to lie on when all the bedding is eaten!

Wood shavings make good bedding for a pony, and are particularly useful for greedy animals that will eat any type of straw bedding. Odd blocks of wood should be picked out of the shavings if they are present. The same applies to sawdust which can be used instead. It is not as good a material as shavings, and tends to heat up as soon as it gets soiled and a little damp, which can damage the animal's feet. Particular care has to be taken to keep sawdust clean and dry, and maintaining an ample supply is necessary. It is generally economical in terms of cost since, like wood shavings, it is frequently available at no cost from many lumberyards.

Shredded paper can also be used as bedding, but may be expensive. Like shavings and sawdust, it is useful when consumption of bedding is a problem. When bedded-up fresh, all these materials are good for ponies that are allergic to molds in straw. In deep litter they have no advantage.

Keeping the Stable Clean

A pony is quite a large animal and its diet (hay and grass) contains a considerable amount of material that it is unable to digest. Consequently, large quantities of manure and urine are produced, which soil the bedding. The manure and the wet bedding should be removed daily—or "mucked out"—and the bedding made up again with fresh supplies. This is probably preferable to the deep litter system, where soiled bedding is allowed to build up gradually, and a thick layer of new straw is added to the top to provide a warm bed for the pony. This deep litter has one advantage, in that it requires less attention each day, though in other respects it is less satisfactory.

Daily mucking out of the stable is an unpleasant task, not least because of the strong smell which impregnates the clothes and footwear of the operator. If you would rather everyone did not know just what you have been doing, coveralls and barn boots are suggested. The unsoiled straw is first sorted with a pitchfork and stacked in a dry corner of the stall. Dirty bedding and manure are loaded into a wheelbarrow to be carted away; for this purpose a manure fork and a shovel are useful. Finally, the floor of the stable is swept clean with a stiff broom. It may be necessary to throw a bucket of water over the floor or hose it down to complete the cleaning process. This will also flush out drains, which tend to get blocked very easily with fragments of straw or other bedding.

The bedding should be left loosely piled in one corner of the stall for several hours, to give it a chance to dry, and to allow the floor to dry and air out. During this time the windows and door should be left open. This is only possible if the pony is turned out for the day or night; otherwise it may be necessary to put the bedding down again right away, whether the floor is wet or not.

Disposal of Manure

Horse manure, particularly that from straw bedding, is an excellent garden fertilizer which helps to compensate for the cost of the straw. Before being applied to the garden, the manure needs to be well rotted. During the rotting process a manure pile will shrink, helping to reduce the volume of material to be disposed of. The way the pile is stacked influences the rotting process.

Manure should be stacked in a heap which has a flat top and vertical sides, the material being spread evenly on the top and leveled off. The purpose of this is to ensure that rainwater soaks into it, rather than running off a pile with sloping sides, as water is essential to the rotting process. This is also improved by the addition of potassium nitrate or some other composting agent. This type of vertical-sided stack also looks neater than an untidy, sprawling heap. To help keep the manure pile square or rectangular a two- or three-sided frame can be constructed of vertical sheets of corrugated iron nailed to posts two or three feet high. A better alternative can be built from concrete blocks.

Fig. 13. Horse manure is a very useful garden fertilizer when it is allowed to rot in a proper manure pile.

The manure stack should be located some distance from the stable itself, so that no odor is noticeable in the building. A hard path of concrete, bricks or—at the very minimum—a series of wooden planks, is usually necessary if the daily passage of a full wheelbarrow of manure is not to make the track unpleasantly muddy in winter.

Making the Pony's Bed

To lay the clean straw into a comfortable bed for a pony is not simply a matter of kicking the bedding over the floor. This will result in it being scattered in lumps, thickly here and thinly there. The bedding should be spread out with a fork so that it makes a level surface with some extra banking up against the walls of the stall. The purpose of this is to prevent drafts blowing around the pony's legs and to avoid the animal becoming trapped, or cast, between the wall and a mound of bedding in the middle of the stall when he lies down.

To make a new bed for a stable 10 feet square, about 50 to 70 pounds of straw are required (most bales are about 60 to

80 pounds or more). The amount varies considerably depending on the quality and type of bedding used and the size of the pony. To reduce the amount of straw put down initially is actually false economy. This seems to increase rather than decrease the amount of bedding which has to be thrown out because it is soiled, as well as increasing the risk of injury to the pony.

Generally between 10 to 20 pounds of new bedding have to be added daily to replace dirty material. Less is required if the pony is out for some of the time. The new straw is usually added at night, and it requires careful shaking out to disentangle the leaves of the bale. The baling wire or twine should be taken off carefully and removed from the stable to prevent the pony from eating it, or getting tangled up in it. Ideally, spreading new straw should be done when the pony is not in the stable, as it takes twenty minutes for dust and mold spores to settle down again afterwards.

If a pony is kept in the stable for a majority of the time it may be necessary to remove only the piles of manure once or twice a day, besides mucking out each morning. This helps to keep the stable clean and sweet-smelling, and prevents the manure being trampled into the bedding. The manure can be removed with a pitchfork and placed in a manure basket, which is emptied onto the manure pile. This is a plastic container with rope handles that can be kept hanging with the other stable cleaning implements. These can be stored on nails driven into the wall, and should include a broom, manure fork, and a shovel. A wire rake is also useful for clearing areas which are not surfaced.

Deep Litter

As an alternative to the thorough daily mucking-out of the stable, a "deep litter" system may be adopted. This involves only the removal of droppings each day, the wet straw being allowed to build up beneath a thick layer of dry. It is sometimes thought that the use of this deep litter method saves bedding material. This is not so, as enough fresh litter has to be added each day to ensure that the animal has a dry surface to lie on. Time spent on the pony each day is saved, however. There is the advantage that whoever looks after the pony does not have clothes and hair impregnated with the scent of the animal. This can be helpful if you are trying to persuade someone else to care for the pony while you are away. The litter does have to be cleaned out completely every few months. This is a large and not particularly pleasant task.

This deep litter may have an advantage, from the pony's point of view, in that it provides a warmer bed than a sparsely littered, daily-cleaned stable. The deep litter itself may produce a little warmth. From the owner's point of view the warm, moist, rotting

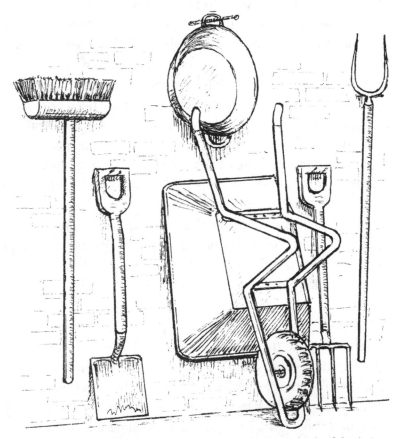

Fig. 14. Stable cleaning equipment: broom, shovel, manure basket (plastic basket with handles), wheelbarrow, manure fork, and pitchfork. The tools are hung on nails driven into the wall.

litter may damage the stable walls with continuous contact, particularly if these are of wood. Some bedding materials are also unsuitable for deep litter; among them are sawdust and shredded newspaper.

Ponies That Eat Their Bedding

Most ponies will pick over fresh straw bedding and consume any odd tasty stalks they find. This does no harm provided they do not eat too much straw. Some animals will, however, eat straw in large quantities—so much that it becomes injurious—a vice.

There are a number of reasons for this tendency. One is just plain hunger. The pony is simply not getting enough other food. The remedy here is obvious. These ponies are often in poor

Fig. 15. Most ponies pick over fresh bedding.

physical condition because not enough attention is being paid to the quantity and quality of hay that is being fed.

Another reason is the quite common one of greed; an already chubby pony gobbling up anything that is possibly edible. To prevent this, the pony may be bedded on newspaper, wood shavings, or sawdust. If straw has to be used, it may be sprinkled with a strong-smelling disinfectant. Mixing the fresh straw with that remaining from the previous day also helps to deter this behavior.

Occasionally a pony may develop a bizarre appetite, consuming bedding of any sort, and maybe even its own manure. Such quirks are sometimes due to heavy infestation with worms, particularly in the young animal, or to a mineral deficiency. Both these situations require consulting your veterinarian.

Boredom may make a pony eat the bedding for amusement. Confined alone for most of the day with nothing to eat but the daily hay and grain ration, is this really surprising? Any animal benefits from having a stable with a view into a yard or area where people and animals are coming and going. The company of another pony, or other stable companion also helps the bored animal, as does being turned out for a few hours a day. As with all so-called "vices," it is better to spend some time trying to work out *why* the pony eats the bedding. This is preferable to spending time and effort trying to prevent the vice by putting on a muzzle, or tying the pony up for hours on end, or changing to less palatable bedding.

Chapter Six

EQUIPPING THE STABLE

Now you have got a suitable building for the pony, equipped with a door and window to permit access and ventilation, plus a warm dry bed for the animal to lie on. The next considerations are the stable fittings and tools. These include such items as water buckets, feed buckets, and hay nets—the essentials which contain the pony's day to day necessities.

Water Container

The type of trough most suitable for the field has already been described, and would be far too big to use in the stable. Indoors, the pony's water can be provided in a bucket, which has the great advantage of being easy to clean. *To thrive, a pony must have a constant supply of fresh water.* The water bucket should be checked and topped up if necessary at least three times a day, though you should automatically check the water supply every time you go into the stable. Every morning, if the pony is in, the water bucket should be emptied, rinsed out, and refilled, as animals seem to dislike water which has stood around overnight. It is best to remove the water bucket from the stable while the box is being mucked out, so that small pieces of soiled material do not get into it. These, understandably, make the water undrinkable.

Scrubbing out the water bucket and rinsing it out thoroughly once a week also helps to ensure that the water is palatable. If this is not done, a slight slime sometimes develops on the inside of the bucket. This appears regardless of the material from which the bucket is made. In this regard there is little difference between galvanized iron, rubber, and heavy plastic. Whatever it is made of, the bucket needs to be solid so that it will not be split by a casual blow from a hoof. It should have a capacity of at least two gallons. If this is too heavy for you to carry when full, you may find it easier to make several journeys with a smaller bucket to fill it up.

The pony's water bucket is generally placed in a corner of the stall, normally by the door and preferably where it will not get full of hay, nor where the pony is likely to foul it. Some ponies, fortunately not many, develop the bad habit of playing football with the water bucket, consequently soaking the bedding and breaking the bucket. For these animals, a hook attached to the wall into which the bucket fits may solve the problem.

An automatic water dish connected to the main water supply is the ideal way to ensure the pony has access to water at all times—avoiding any problems that might occur as a result of water deprivation. Disadvantages are: they are hard to clean, can freeze in cold weather, and may become jammed with hay or bedding, so they must be checked twice a day to ensure they are functioning properly.

Mangers

Very important to any pony is the container in which the meals are given, in particular the pellets or other grains. There has been long-standing argument as to whether it is better for ponies to eat from ground level, as they would naturally do, or from a raised manger or feed bucket that cannot be kicked over. In practice, it seems that the height from which a pony feeds is of little importance, provided it is not below floor level, or higher than about 30 inches above the ground.

Feeding at floor level is certainly the simplest method as the pony is given his meal in a bucket or bowl which is removed when he has finished. These containers have the advantage of being easy to rinse out and keep clean. If you feed the pony from a bucket, do remember two things. First, that there should be no sharp projections from the attachments of the bucket's handle on which the pony might injure himself or catch his halter. Second, that the base of the bucket should be wide enough to allow the pony's nose to reach to the bottom in comfort. Otherwise it can be very distressing if the animal cannot reach all the food.

A more shallow, larger feed dish is really preferable to a bucket, because it enables an animal to get at the feed more easily and see what it is. It is also harder to tip over.

Some ponies persistently paw the ground as they eat, and often knock over their feed bowl so that food is wasted. For them, a manger attached to the wall is the best solution. It is possible to buy triangular plastic or galvanized iron mangers which can be fixed neatly into the corner of the stable. They are easy to clean and, just like any other container, do need an occasional scrub.

Salt Licks

Most ponies appreciate a lump of salt they can lick while they stand in the stable or shelter. Salt can be provided in the field but, being soluble, it is washed away by rain, so it is better kept indoors. It can be provided quite easily as a rectangular block which slides into a special metal holder screwed to the wall. The

Fig. 16. A pony appreciates a salt lick.

most suitable height for this depends on the size of the pony, but usually about 3 to 3½ feet above the ground is comfortable.

This supply of extra salt is not essential to the animal's survival, but most ponies have a natural craving for salt, which they may satisfy by eating earth or chewing on wooden stalls and fences if no salt is available. The two elements of salt, sodium and chlorine, are vital to all living things. The pony's normal daily requirement is supplied in his food, but very hard work, which causes sweating and consequent loss of salt, means that extra may be needed. With a salt lick, the pony can take what he requires.

Feeding Hay

In old stables, a hayrack was always provided. This was usually fixed to the wall several feet above the ground, with the horse pulling down the hay when it was wanted. This method reduced waste but had one disadvantage. As the hay was pulled down, small particles of dry grass and dust were scattered into the animal's eyes and nostrils. It is, therefore, now considered incorrect to feed hay from a container above the horse's head.

The natural way of feeding is to give the pony hay in a pile on the ground. Unfortunately this leads to waste, as the animal tends to pick over the hay, eating the most delicious stalks first and trampling on the rest. This can be avoided by giving the hay in an open-topped rack 2 or 3 feet above the ground, so that the less tasty bits simply fall to the bottom and are not trampled under foot. Such a rack is, however, expensive, and requires proper installation. It also takes up considerable space even when empty. In a loose stall this is more of a disadvantage than in a straight stall, where it is common for a manger, a hayrack, and a holder for a water bucket to be combined in one fixture along the front wall.

A justifiably popular method of feeding hay to ponies is in hay nets. Made of thick string or nylon, the net is stuffed with hay and then tied to a ring in the wall of the stable or, if used outside,

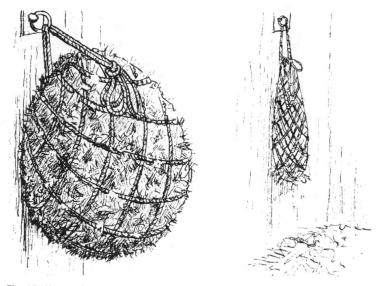

Fig. 17. How to hang a hay net so that it does not dangle on the ground when it is empty.

to a strong fence. It should be secured as shown in fig. 17, with the end of the cord tied to the bottom of the net. This keeps the net from sagging as the hay is eaten, preventing the pony pawing at the empty net and getting its feet caught up in it.

Storing the Pony's Food

Hay and grain are expensive, and therefore deserve proper storage. There is also the serious risk that any type of food that has been poorly stored, and allowed to become damp and moldy, may give the pony colic.

Hay should be stored in a dry building out of reach of the pony. The building may be open sided, and should be well ventilated, with the hay stacked to allow plenty of air circulation.

Straw or other bedding is bulky, and is usually stacked alongside the hay. If you have enough storage space, it is often most economical and less trouble to buy a whole winter's supply of hay and straw in the autumn. Use a reputable supplier who, though he might charge a little more, is unlikely to supply bad material since he has his reputation to consider.

When stored, hay should always be kept neat and tidy. Use up hay and straw bale by bale, so that you do not have several half-used bales lying loose on the floor getting dirty. Most bales are tied with string or wire. Your penknife, scissors, or wire cutters are less likely to get lost if they are fitted with a loop of string so that they can be kept hung up. When you first open a new bale, pick out the string or wire and hang it safely out of the way, on a hook put up specially for this purpose. A useful addition to the hay storage area is a scale, preferably large enough to weigh up to about 20 pounds. This will enable you to check just how much your pony is eating.

Concentrate feeds are supplied in paper, plastic, or burlap bags, but paper and burlap bags are not damp-proof and will not provide a sufficient barrier against rats or mice. So, some kind of dry vermin-proof container is needed to store grain. Proper feed bins can be expensive, but a metal or plastic garbage can (preferably a new one) or an unused chest freezer make satisfactory alternatives. A crafty pony can knock off a garbage can lid to get at the food, but the animal should never have access to the feed storage area anyway. Remember that ponies have died as a result of gorging themselves on grain.

This storage area is also a good place to keep feed and water buckets. You should also have one or more feed scoops which hold a known amount of each type of feed and can be used to measure a set amount into a pony's feed bucket. This helps to ensure that the pony consistently gets its correct ration. A scoop holding one pound of oats (a volume of about one and a half pints) is suitable.

Tying Up the Pony

A tethering ring in the stable is useful not only for hanging up the hay net, but for tying up the pony as well. When you are grooming, for example, or checking the shoes, it is essential that the pony is tethered securely. The tethering ring itself consists of a metal ring attached to the wall about 4 feet from the ground. When tied, the pony's leadrope should be tied to a small loop of baling twine attached to the ring. This cord will break and release the pony if it becomes frightened and panics for some reason, reducing the risk of injury.

Halters are also essential stable equipment. This is a harness of leather or nylon strapping which fits the pony's head. It does not have a bit and can be worn when the pony is loose in the field. It should fit comfortably, so that the noseband does not interfere with the jaws as the pony chews, though it should not be so large that it flaps freely or slips off. A leather halter is an expensive item; one of nylon is not usually so costly.

When it is tied up, a pony should have sufficient rope to allow for movement of the head, but not enough to allow the forelegs to become entangled. The knot used for tying animals

A halter and rope . . .

. . . or a makeshift halter

Fig. 18. A halter and leadrope; or a makeshift one can be made from any handy rope or strap.

should always be the quick-release type—a half-hitch with a loop through it (see fig. 19, below)—so that a jerk on the free end releases the animal. This is very important since ponies are inclined to panic if anything goes wrong. By pulling back hard on the rope, the knot by which the animal is tied can be drawn so tight that it is impossible to undo if it is not of the quick-release type. Sometimes there is a problem with a more cunning pony which has learned to undo this type of knot by pulling the free end with its teeth. This may be discouraged by passing the free end back through the loop again; it means that the knot

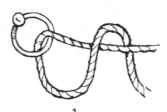

1

2

3

4

5

Fig. 19. Tying up a pony. Steps 1 through 4 show how to tie a quick-release knot. To release the knot, pull the free end. For ponies that learn to undo the knot themselves, the free end can be pulled through the loop as in no. 5.

takes a moment longer to untie in an emergency, but it still will not pull up tight.

In a loose stall a pony is unlikely to be tied up for long periods and is generally tied directly to a tethering ring. In a straight stall, however, there can be a problem. The animal requires enough rope to lie down comfortably, but with this length of rope dangling from its head, the pony is likely to get tangled up.

And Outside . . .

Outside the stable there are a number of fittings which can make life easier. A hook by the stable door, for example, provides somewhere to keep the pony's halter. Then there can be no excuse for just dumping it on the ground when the pony is in its stall, or for leading the animal around by the mane because a halter isn't handy. Hooks are also necessary to fasten back doors and windows so that they do not swing in the wind.

A water faucet near the stable door is convenient, reducing the distance water has to be carried, and making it possible to hose down flooring. All stable work is made easier if the building has a small gravel or paved area outside. In winter you do not want to wade through a sea of mud every time you go in and out. If the stable is not already situated in a field, a fence around the area will prevent the pony from straying too far if he should get loose. This is particularly important near a road.

Fire!

Fire in a stable is a scene of horror. It is all too easy to be lulled into a sense of false security, of "it could never happen to us." Unfortunately fire can, and does, break out anywhere.

Some buildings are in particular danger from fire. Many fires start as sparks from faulty electrical wiring. Whatever materials they are constructed from, all stables have dry hay and straw in them and both of these materials burn very well, so a very strict no-smoking rule is a must.

If a fire should break out, the first thing to remember is not to panic. That never helps anyone. If the fire is small, rapidly douse it with cold water—a bucketful is better than nothing, and a pressure hose is better still. If the fire is bigger, first warn any other people in the building, and then remove any animals. Ponies and dogs are best tied securely, well out of the way. As soon as possible contact the fire department by telephone.

A fire extinguisher is a good investment, and should be kept somewhere obvious and easily accessible. It could make the difference between a building being destroyed and being saved. However, a fire extinguisher does have quite an important snag; namely, that some young pony owners may find it too heavy to lift or point at the fire. For their use, a hose permanently fitted to the water faucet may be much more satisfactory, as long as it doesn't freeze up.

Chapter Seven

GRASS AS PONY FOOD

The best feed for a pony is grass. Not only is it their natural food, grazing also provides the animal with continuous occupation and exercise. But even though grazing may be the pony's natural way of life, simply being turned loose in a paddock and left to fend for itself is not the best way to keep the animal in first-class condition throughout the year.

One important reason for this is that grass grows well only when there is sufficient moisture, warmth, and sunlight. Its nutritive value therefore varies greatly from season to season. In the wild, a pony could probably find enough to keep going during hard times in winter and early spring. A domesticated animal is in a different position, and, enclosed in a small field, has less opportunity to search for edible material when grass is short. Through the winter months, from about November to May, your pony requires extra food in the form of hay and perhaps "concentrates"—grain and pelleted feed.

In early summer the situation is reversed. The winter shortage of grass is replaced by plenty, and quite often excess. Especially in May, grass is highly nutritious, and ponies which have free access to it tend to become overly fat and lazy and may also suffer diseases of obesity, such as laminitis, also known as founder. At this time of year the pony may have to be shut away from the grass for part of each day to ensure protection from the ill effects of such indulgence.

The Grazing Pony's Day
A pony living out on grass tends to settle into a fixed routine, which is seldom broken unless disturbed by humans. The animal

will probably graze for between sixteen and eighteen hours each day, though this depends to some degree on the quality of the grass available. Later in the summer, the feed value of the pasture decreases, and the pony's intake has to increase to compensate. On an average day a midsized pony will eat 50 to 75 pounds of grass.

Most eating is done in the few hours just after dawn, and in the period before dusk, when dew is still on the grass. A pony seldom does much grazing while it is actually dark. In winter, when days are short, grazing time is reduced—another reason why supplementary feeding is so important at this time. In the early morning the pony grazes hard for a couple of hours and will then have a short rest, perhaps a drink at the water trough, and may lie down for a little while and doze. Later in the day quite a bit of time may be spent in what could be called casual grazing, moving about the field at random, and picking, rather than eating continuously.

This tendency to pick helps account for the reputation horses have as bad grazers. They are inclined to eat all of the most tasty grasses, leaving the ones they do not like to grow tall and rank. Cattle graze much more evenly. Having no top teeth, they have to tear out the grass in bunches instead of biting it off neatly as horses do. In fact, the pony's excellent incisors, or front teeth, allow it not only to cleanly bite off of the blades of grass, but also to bite them almost to the ground. This is why grass takes a long time to recover from being grazed by horses.

Having spent most of the daytime roaming around the paddock and grazing, the pony usually settles down to spend the night in some suitable sheltered place. In summer it may be warm enough to lie down to rest; in winter it is usually too cold and wet for this.

If the pony is stabled for part of the time, this behavior pattern is modified. If kept stabled for most of the day in summer—to avoid flies and excessive heat, for instance—the animal may have to spend the night grazing and rely on being able to lie down and rest in its stall by day, so that some fresh bedding will be appreciated.

Stabling the pony at night in winter is unlikely to alter grazing behavior noticeably. The animal will probably take advantage of comfortable bedding in the stable to lie down and rest.

The Paddock

Ponies are generally good at living on fairly meager rations by the comparison with, for example, a dairy cow producing thousands of gallons of milk a year. Most equines do best on a moderate, though adequate, diet. Very rich pastures are not ideal for a pony, and grazing of medium quality is best. However, this is not meant to imply that a pony will survive on a patch of bare earth with nothing growing on it but a sea of weeds.

A medium-quality pasture is one which contains a fair proportion of more nutritionally valuable grasses, such as perennial rye grass, timothy, fescue, and white clover. Mixed in with these will be less useful grasses. Weeds, such as thistles, nettles, goldenrod, and burdock may also be present. Though these are not directly harmful, they take up space and light which could instead produce something more valuable. Broad-leaved weeds, such as nettles and thistles, can be controlled by spraying with weedkiller (though this should be done only when the pony is being kept elsewhere) or by cutting weeds before they go to seed. If the weed problem gets really out of hand, there may be nothing else to do but get the paddock plowed and reseeded with a good grass mixture.

Poisonous weeds are more of a problem, and it is worth keeping an eye on what is growing in the paddock. Some apparently harmless trees and plants cause unexpected problems. Oak trees, for example, can shed large numbers of acorns after a windy day in the fall. If eaten in large quantities by a hungry or greedy pony, acorns can cause serious, sometimes fatal, illness.

Yew is a very poisonous shrub and causes a large proportion of the cases of poisoning of grazing animals. Particularly after a storm there is a risk that branches will have blown off and wilted, and at this time the animals seem more ready to eat them. If there are any questionable plants growing in the field, the wisest precaution is to remove them completely so that none are within reach of a pony or any other livestock.

Prompt removal of uprooted weeds is very important, for most poisonous plants seem to become more attractive to animals as they wilt. This is true of much other vegetation as well. Besides their increased palatability if they are allowed to wilt, poisonous plants may occasionally attract a very hungry animal or one with an altered appetite as a result of excessive worm infestation or because of mineral deficiency.

Overgrazed Pasture

The bad effect of ponies on grassland has already been mentioned. The tendency of these animals to bite some areas bare, yet leave others to grow rank and coarse, may suggest to the owners of ponies—incorrectly—that while there is long grass on the field there is plenty for a pony to eat. But the animal would much sooner go hungry than eat this tough vegetation.

Another reason for these patchy grazing habits is that ponies tend to deposit droppings only in certain areas and, naturally, will not graze around their own manure. Cows have no such dislike and if turned out in the same field will level the grass in a field very well; alternatively, patches of very long grass can be cut with a mowing machine to encourage new growth. The ideal solution, if time permits, is to pick up the droppings and remove them.

In some respects the strong tendency of a pony to avoid grazing near droppings is an advantage, as it may help to reduce the numbers of worm parasites which are acquired. Small worms can inhabit the pony's gut, where they live on any food passing through. Their presence reduces the benefits the animal derives from its food and may lead to weakness and poor condition. Worms produce vast numbers of microscopic eggs which pass out in the animal's droppings. Protected from the destructive effects of cold weather and sunlight by the heap of fecal matter,

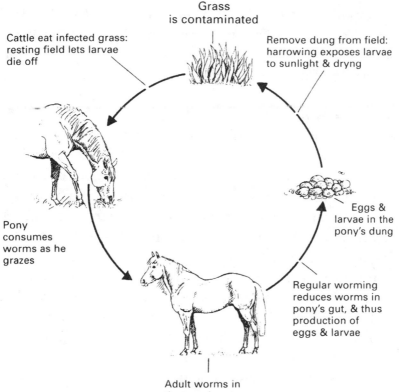

Grass
is contaminated

Cattle eat infected grass:
resting field lets larvae
die off

Remove dung from field:
harrowing exposes larvae
to sunlight & dryng

Pony
consumes
worms as he
grazes

Eggs &
larvae in the
pony's dung

Regular worming
reduces worms in
pony's gut, & thus
production of
eggs & larvae

Adult worms in
the pony's gut

Fig. 20. The life cycle of a pony's parasites. The breaks in the line show the methods by which this cycle can be broken

the eggs develop quickly to a state where they are able to infect any pony, especially a young one, which consumes them in the course of grazing or feeding. The eggs simply die if eaten by an animal of another species, so that cattle grazing with a pony would not be affected. Similarly, there is little risk of a pony being infected with cattle worms.

A pasture which has had horses or ponies on it for a long time, and has been poorly maintained, becomes a dangerous source of worm eggs, as well as developing the characteristically patchy growth of grass. This condition is sometimes called "horse-sick." Apart from keeping cattle in the field for a time, or mowing the areas of long grass, regular harrowing to disperse the manure and expose parasites to light and cold is also valuable. It is vital that all ponies in a field are wormed regularly and simultaneously. This must be done to prevent dangerous levels of contamination of the pasture with parasites developing.

Area per Pony

Resting grazing land regularly is important. If you can, divide the field into two halves and let the animals graze them alternately, rather than letting them run over the whole area all the time. The grass in each half is given a chance to recover, and while it is empty a large portion of parasites on the grass will also perish, thus reducing that problem, too.

If the pasture is of average quality, not too lush but not overly sparse either, then one pony should be able to live off one and a half to two acres, plus some supplemental feed in the winter. The quality of the grass, the way it is managed, how much fertilizer is spread on it, and so on, all have a bearing on what proportion of the pony's food comes from the field.

The best indicator of the quality of the grass is the condition of the animal. Ponies that are sleek, alert, and reasonably plump are probably getting enough to eat. If yours looks miserable, with its coat staring, and the body thin and "tucked up," then it is time you increased its rations. The season of the year affects the amount of grass that grows. Is the winter unusually hard, or unexpectedly mild? Is the spring abnormally late? These factors alter the condition of a pony living on grass, so that supplementary feeding has to be modified accordingly.

In the early summer there may be an abundance of grass available and even a field as small as one and three-quarter acres will probably provide enough food to make a pony overweight. During this period it is usually necessary to restrict the food intake. This can be done either by shutting the pony in a stable during the daytime—where it will have the added advantage of being away from the flies—or by running other ponies or cattle on the field to help eat down the grass.

Alternatively, part of the field can be fenced off with an electric fence. One part may be used to make some hay of your own to feed the pony during the winter. However, making good hay is not all that easy and there is a risk that you might end up with only a moldy, damp product which could be worse for the pony than nothing at all. If you decide to try to get some hay off the paddock, it is worth asking a local farmer to do the hard work for you. He probably would be willing to advise you on care of the pasture, too.

Catching the Pony

Most ponies seem to enjoy being free in a grassy paddock; most are also good and reliably easy to catch. A pony is far easier to catch if it was left already wearing a halter. Then all you have to do is to carry the leading rope in your pocket or behind your back and walk up to the animal. Talking as you approach helps. Develop the habit of always taking a treat when you go into the field, whether you intend catching the pony or not. This gets the idea ingrained that you always bring something edible. The pony is then concentrating on the food you are bringing and

Fig. 21. The pony is concentrating on the food that you are bringing.

thoughts do not turn to running away. Walk up, give the treat, gently pat its neck, and quietly hook the lead onto the halter, ready to lead the pony to the gate.

Unfortunately, things do not always work out as smoothly as this, and the pony may decide to play hard to get. This is more likely if you approach noisily or hurriedly, or if the pony is not expecting a bribe in the form of a tidbit or a handful of oats in the bottom of a bucket. Ponies which are hard to catch anyway are always more difficult if they are not turned out with a halter on.

There are few things more irritating than a pony which tries to avoid being caught, particularly if you have been looking forward to a trail ride on a glorious summer morning, and even more so if you had intended going to a show or group ride. The possibility that you may not be able to catch the animal when desired is one good reason for shutting a pony in overnight before such occasions. The best immediate solution to the problem is probably to leave the pony for half an hour, and then return with some feed in a bucket. Few ponies can resist the prospect of a delicious meal. It is important that you do not allow yourself to become impatient, as the animal will sense this very quickly and it will only make things worse.

In the long run, visiting the pony frequently in the field, always taking along a treat, will get your pony into the habit of looking to see what you have brought. For a really difficult animal, give a small feeding of grain at the same time each day, whether you intend to go for a ride or not. This will get the pony into the habit of coming to the gate to meet you, and used to being stroked and petted. It is a good policy to catch the pony daily anyway so that you can look the animal over for injuries or illness, and to check that it has sufficient water available.

Hay and Grass

Hay is grass which is cut and allowed to dry in the sun when the weather is hot and dry. The grass itself is of high nutritive value as it comes into flower. The quality of hay depends on two factors: the type of grass from which it is made, and the timing, with regard to the weather, of the haymaking process. This also includes correct stacking.

The best quality hay has not been rained on while lying out in the field. Good hay is sweet smelling with no trace of mold or mustiness, and is slightly green in color. The quality of the hay determines its value—or its worthlessness—as a feed for your pony. To buy poor hay is false economy, as you will have to feed much more of it, as well as subjecting the animal to various health risks (especially COPD). Recently made hay should never be fed to horses as it can cause serious digestive problems. Ideally, hay should be stacked for six months before use. In the fall, hay made the previous summer should be used if possible. When new hay is first fed, it should be introduced gradually, and mixed in with older hay for a few days.

The amount of hay has to vary inversely with the amount and quality of the grazing a pony is getting, and according to the animal's condition. It depends also, but to a lesser degree, on the amount of work which is done, and the amount of other feed you are giving. Hay is really a pony's staple food in winter, in the same way that grass is in summer, and should not be reduced, whatever the state of your finances. It also has the great advantage, particularly for young riders, that ponies can consume and enjoy large quantities of good quality hay without getting too frisky.

As a rough guide, during the winter a pony of about 12.2 hh requires 5 to 9 pounds of good hay daily, a 13.2 hh pony 6 to 11 pounds and a 14.2 hh pony 8 to 12 pounds daily. This does, however, assume that there is also access to good pasture. If the pony is stabled, or on very poor pasture, or the ground is covered with snow and frost, the hay requirement would be about doubled, and the animal would need supplemental feed. It is necessary to feed hay from about mid-October until the middle or end of April. It is never worth delaying this change in the interest of saving money, because this means that the pony begins the cold-weather season rather thin and run down just when it needs to be really fit and well. The result will be bigger feed bills overall, apart from the pony's suffering. Gross underfeeding can amount to cruelty.

If the grazing in your pony's paddock is very sparse, it may also be necessary to feed hay in summer. As an alternative, you may prefer to feed cut grass. So long as you feed only really fresh grass this is unlikely to do any harm, though you should be sure to remove any wilted material. This is liable to give the animal colic, particularly if the grass has decomposed so far that it has begun to heat up. Lawn clippings are extraordinarily dangerous as they ferment very rapidly especially when raked into a pile. Also, being relatively fine, they can tend to cause an impaction in the pony's stomach, especially if the animal is greedy and swallows them rapidly without chewing them. Large quantities of lawn mowings should therefore be added to the compost pile, and not given to the pony.

Chapter Eight

EXTRA FOOD

The outdoor pony eats grass in the summer, and in winter eats the same thing in the form of the hay, which is given instead. Grass is the most natural food, but if the pony is working hard or the weather is bad there will be a need for something besides grass and hay to give energy and warmth. The extra feed should be provided by grain or one of the wide variety of other pony foods which—being less bulky than grass and hay—are collectively called "concentrates."

These foods are usually given in a bucket, manger, or feed bowl. This is an artificial form of feeding, very different from the pony's natural way of eating. Further, the equine digestive system is very easily upset. Incorrectly fed, concentrates can produce colic, a severe stomachache with serious, and potentially fatal, complications. If the pony is intended to derive maximum benefit from extra food (as well as the most enjoyment) without any risk to its health, it has to be fed with skill and care. The following ten are the most important principles of feeding.

Feed Plenty of Roughage
In the wild, a pony eats grass, and lots of it. The domesticated pony also needs the fiber that grass or hay provides. Digestion is more efficient if the pony has to chew food thoroughly. The gut of herbivores is adapted to function best if it is always full of roughage, which brings us to the next point . . .

Give Small Feeds Often
A pony's eating habits differ from those of a human being. We prefer to eat our food in three or four daily meals. Dogs carry

this still further, for they will happily eat just one colossal meal a day, or even one every couple of days. This is partly because dogs have stomachs which will stretch enormously. A pony, by contrast, has only a very small and inelastic one, so it eats steadily and most of the time, stopping only for an occasional nap, or when taken out for a ride.

If the pony goes without food for a long time and then gobbles a large meal, the stomach is stretched severely and may not be able to hold all the food, which can result in a form of colic. For a pony living indoors all the time, the daily ration should be divided into at least three feeds, and preferably four, per day. A pony living outdoors may get only one feeding of grain per day, plus hay, but is eating grass for much of the rest of the time.

Feed Good Food Only

Ponies do not thrive on poor quality, old, stale or moldy food, and it may actually do them serious harm. Many animals will not eat it, but occasionally a pony gobbles up, for example, moldy hay. As a result the unfortunate animal may spend an uncomfortable night, and the owner may as well. Poor quality feed also has little nutritive value. It may be cheaper to buy in the first place, but you will have to feed much more to get the same result. The cost is the same, or even more, in the long run.

Feed According to Exercise

Ponies are very good at regulating their own intake of hay. After eating a certain quantity there is simply no room for more, so the rest is left, though it may be eaten later. This is one of the reasons why hay is such a valuable food for ponies and one with which, provided it is of good quality, it is hard to make serious mistakes in feeding.

The most common concentrates fed to horses are crimped or rolled oats, sweet feed, cracked corn, sugar beet pulp, and various types of complete pelleted rations. These provide the energy needed to keep the pony warm in the cold weather, to perform work, and to improve a pony's condition if it is rather thin or so poor that it needs energy just to live. Thus it is reasonable that in very cold weather or when being ridden a lot, especially in winter, a pony needs concentrates as well as hay and grass.

There are one or two exceptions to this. Concentrates can tend to make a very small pony unmanageable unless he is being worked especially hard. It is unwise to give too much sweet feed or corn to a pony that is already misbehaving or difficult to cope with. An adequate ration of good quality hay and perhaps some oats is usually sufficient for such animals. Occasionally a few pellets may be fed—if the weather is very bad, for example—as these do not seem to have the exciting effect of most other feeds.

Feed According to Condition

The drains being made on the pony's energy reserves (due to cold weather, hard work, illness) give you an idea of roughly how much you should feed in the way of concentrates. The condition of the pony allows you to make fine adjustments to the food. If the animal is looking well, seems full of energy, is alert and interested, with a shiny coat (the winter coat should glisten as well as the summer one) and is reasonably plump (so that you can only just feel the ribs) then the pony is probably being fed about right. If it's being particularly difficult or looking overweight, or both, the pony is probably having too much. The first thing to reduce, or perhaps cut out completely, is the grain ration. The hay or grass intake may be reduced a little, if necessary, later.

If the pony is too thin, on the other hand, something has to be done, in case not enough food is being consumed. A pony is said to be "poor" if ribs are easily visible, the coat is stark and staring, the animal seems to lack energy, vitality, and interest in what is going on around it, and tends to stand "tucked up" (see fig. 22) with its head down, looking thoroughly miserable. A pony may lose condition simply for lack of enough decent food, either because it is not being given, or because other animals in the

Fig. 22. If the pony stands "tucked up" . . .

field are eating that particular animal's share. These problems you can remedy yourself.

There may be no improvement if the pony is in fact eating enough but the teeth have become pointed and inefficient for grinding the food. Or the cause may be infestation with worm parasites, or the pony may be ill. If any of these problems are suspected, the sooner you get your veterinarian to come and have a look at the pony the better.

Fig. 23. Let the pony eat in peace.

Water Before Feed

Ample supplies of good clean water are essential if a pony is to thrive, and it is best if fresh water is available all the time. If for any reason it is not, or if you have just returned from a ride, offer a long drink—as much as the pony wants—before giving the feed. The reason for this is that water passes more rapidly through the front parts of the pony's gut. If feed is there already, a sort of traffic jam is created with the water pushing from behind. The result may be painful for the pony, with a lot of stretching of that sensitive intestine, and the resulting colic may be severe.

Let the Pony Eat in Peace

It is a sound rule to feed the pony last thing before you go indoors yourself. Eating is a very important business to all animals and they hate to be disturbed by people rushing around, grooming them, or moving other animals around. A pony may also, probably without thinking, lash out unexpectedly if touched when eating, so it is best left alone.

If you must watch the animal eat, do so from a good distance, from outside the stable or paddock. It is better to go away, and return half an hour later to see if the food has been finished.

Feed All the Ponies

Ponies' tempers can become very short at feeding times and even the best of friends will kick out viciously at, and possibly even injure, one another when they are milling around. Never feed just one pony, or leave one out when you feed several. This is just asking for trouble. If only one animal is to be fed, take that pony out of the field, and out of the sight and smell of the others, to give this meal. Sometimes one pony has to be left out. This animal should be given a "pretend" feed, a bucket with a small handful of bran or oats, to keep it occupied while the others eat.

Besides providing one feed bucket and one hay net per pony, you should ensure that each bucket and net is out of range of any other pony. If this is not done, a more dominant pony is likely to get double portions, while the shy animal is left without.

Work Before Food

A pony takes one and a half to two hours to digest a full-sized meal and, like you, can get an uncomfortable feeling if strenuous exercise is done on a full stomach. So you should always arrange the feed to be given upon returning from a ride, never just before going out.

Feed in this context includes a period of grazing, or a net of hay, as well as grain. The pony should be shut in without food (only water) for at least an hour before being taken out. If you have absolutely nowhere to enclose or tie the animal away from the grass, then walking slowly for the first forty minutes of your ride will help.

Making a horse gallop when full of food can bring considerable discomfort. Among the signs of distress are labored breathing, excessive sweating, and reluctance to move forward. Abdominal pain may be indicated by kicking at the belly with a hind hoof and looking around suspiciously at the quarters. If distress is severe, try leading the pony around at a walk for twenty minutes or half an hour. If there is no improvement in this time, the vet should be called.

Feeding Routine

All animals prefer to be fed at the same time each day. They soon come to expect their meal then, and are standing at the gate or hanging over their stable doors waiting. Patience may run out if the food is late.

The main feed of concentrates and hay is usually given at night so that the pony has plenty of time to eat and digest it. Since nighttime is the coldest part of the day, the warming effect of feed is of the greatest benefit then, especially to ponies living outdoors. A second feed is best given in the early morning and, for stabled animals, a third is given in the middle of the day and a fourth at about 4 PM. This routine has to be adjusted to suit the timetables of the humans who do the work, and to fit in with the animal's exercise.

If the feeding routine has to be changed, it should be done gradually. This applies both to alterations in the time when the food is given and to changes in the feed itself; for example from oats to cracked corn, or the addition of one or more new ingredients to the diet. The keyword in all these changes is caution, for a pony's digestion can very easily be upset by any drastic change, even to a conventional horse food of good quality.

Oats for Ponies

The traditional grain for horses and ponies is oats, which are given either whole or rolled, by crushing or rolling within a special mill. Both are readily available from feed stores, though whole oats can be crushed before feeding if you have your own milling machine. The nutritive value of the grain begins to deteriorate rapidly at about seven to fourteen days after crushing, so this should be freshly done if possible. A normal, healthy pony with good teeth can chew whole oats as efficiently as crushed ones. The former have the added advantage that you can get a better idea of the quality of the grains. These should be plump and full, with a good bright color and a weight of 40 pounds or more to the bushel. They should be shiny and clean, with no stalks and seeds of weeds or pieces of earth among them.

Avoid oats with thin grains which have little or no room for a kernel, though they will have a huge fiber content, and any batches where there is mold or grayness. This indicates that the grain has been soaked at some time, probably with rain. Chew a grain yourself. It should taste pleasant, not mealy, and be slightly sweet. Oats, like any other grain, should be fed by weight. Most people use a measuring scoop with a capacity that has been established; any small bowl is suitable.

Sugar Byproducts

A byproduct of the extraction of beet sugar is the minced pulp of the beet which is sold for animal feed. Since it is marketed dry, sugar beet pulp must be soaked overnight in an equal volume of water to allow it to swell fully. If this is not done, the swelling will occur either in the pony's esophagus (the food tube in the throat) causing a "choke," or in the pony's stomach and intestines, causing severe colic. Over half of the cases of choke attended by veterinarians are caused by feeding dry sugar beet pulp, usually inadvertently. Still, sugar beet pulp is a useful feed for ponies, providing some roughage plus residual sugar, in itself an energy source. It can be used to supplement or partially to replace a ration of oats or pelleted feed.

Pelleted Feeds

Various concentrated feeds are available that are specially formulated for feeding to horses and ponies. Many different types are sold; some have a high protein and energy content and are really too rich for most ponies. At the other end of the scale are those which contain a high proportion of roughage—fiber—and are designed to be fed as the sole food, with only a little hay or grass. Between these extremes are pellets which comfortably take the place of a mixture of oats and bran and may be fed either mixed with these, mixed with just corn or bran, or on their own. Sweet feeds have added molasses, to make the seed even more palatable.

Alfalfa cubes are more convenient to provide than hay. They are dense squares of compressed and chopped alfalfa hay, which take up little space, and may be simply measured into the manger. They have the advantage of being easy to transport and store, especially when on the road, but the disadvantage of very high cost, and of not providing the animal with the time-consuming entertainment value that hay offers, thus often leading to boredom. This can result in an increased incidence of chewing on stable doors, walls, and fences, and may also encourage ponies to look to any available straw bedding to chew on. They are also very high in protein, and may simply be too rich for the pony's dietary needs.

Though feeding on prepared rations may sound easy, there are pitfalls. One of these is the need for ponies to eat some roughage with, or just before, any pellets, except those high-fiber "complete diet" brands. This is necessary because under an unfortunate combination of circumstances the pellets could possibly pack down into a mudlike mass with which the pony's stomach cannot cope, except with additional roughage. The result could be a severe, or fatal, colic. Such a tragedy is averted by ensuring that the animal never bolts a ration of pellets on an empty stomach. There should always be some roughage, in the form of grazing or hay, provided to pick at before the grain ration.

Bran

Bran is a byproduct of the milling of wheat to produce the flour we eat as bread.

Bran should smell sweet, and should show no signs of sour-ness, lumps, or mold. Though it has some nutritive value, its main use in feed is as a source of roughage. Mix it with oats or pellets in a ratio of about one to three or four. You can also dampen the bran with a sprinkling of cold water, to prevent the pony blowing the loose flakes out of the manger.

Bran may be fed to a pony in another way: as a bran mash. This is, in effect, bran that is partially cooked. It is therefore very digestible, and suitable for a sick or convalescent pony, or one which is tired after a hard day's or week's work. The mash is made by putting about 2 pounds of bran plus a tablespoonful of salt in a bucket and adding to it enough boiling water to saturate it. It is then stirred thoroughly and covered with a cloth or burlap grain sack while it soaks and cools.

Fig. 24. Making a bran mash.
Left: Put about 2 pounds of bran into a bucket.
Center: Add enough boiling water to saturate it.
Right: Cover with a sack and let it stand until it is cool enough to feed to the pony.

Do not feed a bran mash until it has cooled sufficiently for your hand to be immersed comfortably. The bran mash takes time to cool down, usually a couple of hours, and it is important to stir it well before you test the temperature. Pockets of scalding bran may remain, which will give the pony a shock if come upon unexpectedly. A few oats can be sprinkled on the top.

Variety may also be provided by adding carrots or apples—cut carefully into fingers to avoid risk of the pony choking—which are also appreciated. As an occasional treat, a little molasses added to the feed will make it more enjoyable for a pony, as well as more nutritious. This process is particularly good for concealing any medicines which may have been included in the meal.

Chapter Nine

GROOMING YOUR PONY

The desire for a pleasing appearance is not the only reason for grooming a pony. There are other benefits to be gained. One is that in the course of grooming you will go all over the body and you will find, for example, any small injuries, or the beginnings of skin diseases, or problems with the hooves, which require attention.

When you brush the pony before riding, pay particular attention to removing any mud from the areas beneath the saddle, girth, and bridle. If this is not done, gritty particles may be rubbed into the skin by the tack, and cause discomfort and perhaps soreness. Even if you are going for a quick ride and you don't have the time to groom the pony thoroughly, make a point of brushing mud completely from the saddle and girth areas.

A stabled pony, living a confined, indoor life, needs a thorough daily grooming to tone up the whole body. Grooming has a massaging effect, which improves the circulation to the skin and keeps the pony clean. The outdoor pony does not need this daily attention to the coat, though it also benefits from being well groomed whenever ridden.

Grooming Equipment

Grooming includes picking out the pony's feet. For this you need a blunt metal hook, called a *hoof pick*, to remove any dirt or stones lodged in the foot. The dirt is scraped from the foot, beginning at the heel and working towards the toe, taking care to thoroughly clean the grooves on either side of the frog. Picking out your pony's feet should always be the first job done when grooming, to ensure that it is not forgotten. It is a task which should be done before going for a ride and again upon your return, so that any stones are removed before they can damage the foot. If a nail has been picked up or the shoe has become loose, it can be

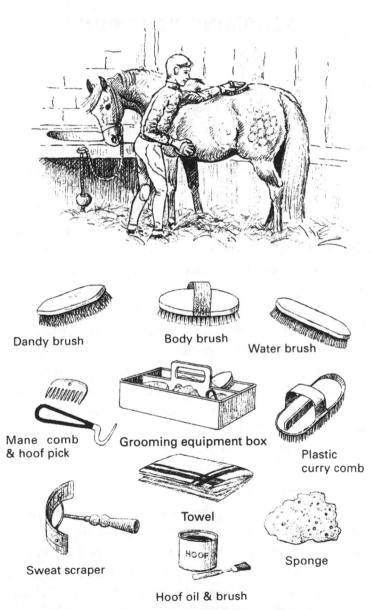

Fig. 25. Grooming the pony; grooming equipment.

noticed and receive prompt attention. Of all the grooming equipment, the hoof pick is probably the most vital.

A *dandy brush* is a stiff brush, often made with nylon bristles set in a wooden back. It is very effective for getting the worst dirt off the pony, particularly mud. It is better not to use a dandy brush on the face, though, as it is somewhat hard. It should not be used on the mane and tail, either, unless they are exceptionally thick, as the stiff bristles will pull out a lot of hair and leave a sparse appearance.

A *body brush* is less hard than the dandy brush and is used to give the pony's body a thorough cleaning, and also to brush the face, mane, and tail. It has shorter, softer bristles than the dandy brush and is used in combination with a *curry comb*. This tool is usually made of metal or hard rubber, with toothed ridges across it. Rub the curry comb over the body brush to clean out the dirt and dander. Dirt that accumulates on the curry comb is cleaned off periodically by tapping one corner of it on a hard floor or a stone, preferably somewhere where the dirt will not be blown straight back onto the clean pony.

The back of the body brush has a loop for the hand to give a better grip so that considerable pressure can be applied. Stand facing the tail. Use the brush in the hand nearest the pony (that is, the brush in the right hand if grooming the left side, and vice versa) and hold the curry comb in the other hand. Brushing in the direction in which the hairs lie, you can really work at the animal's coat to get it clean and make it shine, rubbing the curry comb over the brush every half dozen strokes or so.

A curry comb should not be used on the body of a clipped pony, as it may scratch the skin, and should only be used very gently on a pony with a summer coat. It may be applied more briskly to a pony's heavy winter coat, and can be very useful for removing thick layers of mud. The curry comb should, obviously, never be used on the pony's head, nor the tail and mane, nor on the legs, which, being bony, are easily bruised and scratched. Plastic and rubber curry combs, which are available in a variety of patterns, are very useful for outdoor ponies. These are particularly effective for removing caked mud and sweat from all parts of the pony's body and legs, since they are more flexible.

Now that the pony is clean, it is time to give it a final polish. A *stable rubber*, which is a piece of cloth or a fine towel, can be used to rub over the pony's coat at the end of grooming, to remove dust and give a nice shine. If the pony is entered in a show, its feet may be oiled as a finishing touch. Hoof oil can be obtained from a tack dealer and is applied with a small brush after having scraped or brushed any dried mud from the hooves first. It is best not to wash mud from the feet because repeated wetting of the hoof may lead to soreness around the heels, or cracked heels. It is not necessary to oil a pony's feet routinely. Doing so can interfere with water balance within the hoof, and may contribute to brittle hooves.

A *sponge* is a standard item of grooming equipment. It must be kept clean and should be rinsed out in tap water. When dampened, it is used to gently wipe the pony's eyes and nostrils, and if it is very dirty a different sponge can be used for cleaning under the dock.

A *sweat scraper* is also useful for dealing with a very wet pony, and is essentially a curved piece of metal or rubber attached to a handle. The scraper removes a surprising amount of water when passed over the coat.

A water brush is also sometimes used, and is a soft brush whose purpose it is to dampen the pony's mane and tail to make them lie down neatly. A piece of equipment which is included in any standard grooming kit, but which is seldom used, is the *mane comb*. This is a stout comb, often made of metal. It should never be used on the pony's tail, as it pulls out the hair. It is not wise to comb the mane much either, for the same reason, so that the only times when a mane comb should be used are when braiding a mane or tail, or trimming them.

The grooming kit is easier to keep organized if you use a box or grooming tray to put things in. An old or perhaps leaky bucket makes a good container. All these items should be washed regularly in soap and water, and the brushes and sponge dried thoroughly in the sun or beside a radiator. It is pointless to groom a pony using dirty tools as this could apply more dirt than is removed; It may also increase the risk of skin disease.

Grooming an Outdoor Pony

All ponies love to roll on the ground and they always seem to choose the dirtiest place in the field to do it (particularly if they are grays!). A pony is usually rather muddy when first brought in, even though the coat may be glossy underneath the layer of earth. For grooming, put on a sturdy halter and rope, which should be tied to a suitable ring in the wall or a stout fence with a quick-release knot.

After cleaning out the feet and scraping the worst of the mud from the outside of the hooves with the hoof pick, the next job is to remove the bulk of the mud from the pony's coat, using the dandy brush, and perhaps the curry comb. If the coat is short, it can then be brushed effectively with a body brush, paying special attention to the saddle area. It is sometimes said that a body brush should not be used on an outdoor pony's coat, as it removes natural oil and makes the hair less waterproof. This seems unlikely under normal circumstances. In fact, a thorough grooming probably improves the condition of the coat by enhancing activity of the oil-producing glands of the skin, which is reflected in the hair's glossiness. However, a body brush may have little effect on a shaggy winter coat.

While you have the body brush in your hand, the pony's tail and mane are brushed out from their roots, a lock at a time, so that the hair is cleaned and all tangles removed. This can be a very long job if it is only done occasionally. If the tail and mane are groomed often they lose the twists of hair, or "rats' tails," that may otherwise appear, and become easier to deal with. The pony's face is also brushed with the body brush. To do this the animal is untied and the halter can be buckled loosely around the neck. Holding the rope in one hand, brush the face and fore-lock carefully, and sponge both eyes and nostrils before buckling the halter back in its normal place, and tying the pony up again.

Next comes a final polish for the coat with a clean towel, though this may not be possible if the coat is very long and shaggy, as in winter. In summer, as a finishing touch, you may like to apply some fly repellent onto the horse's skin, which will help to discourage insects from being a nuisance while you are out riding.

In winter, in particular, you may bring the pony in from the field wet. It is impossible to groom the animal in this condi-tion. The quickest way to dry the pony off is in a stable or shelter with plenty of deep bedding. Excessive water is removed first with a sweat scraper, and the pony can then be rubbed thoroughly with clean, dry straw or several towels to further dry it off. An old blanket can be put on and, if necessary, loose stable bandages on the legs, to keep it warm and aid the dry-ing process. If it is especially rainy, as much as an hour may be needed for the pony to dry enough to allow attention with a brush.

Quartering and Washing a Pony

Grooming a stabled pony follows much the same pattern as cleaning an outdoor one, except that there is less time spent removing mud. A full grooming takes about an hour of hard work to do properly. A stabled pony should be thoroughly groomed daily, to keep it in good health, improve circulation, and help compensate for long periods of standing still.

Quartering is the name given to the quick grooming over a stabled pony—or a clean outdoor pony—before going out, for example. The animal is not dirty, and the quartering, with a dandy brush over the body and a body brush to tidy the mane and tail, just makes the pony look presentable. It includes, of course, picking out the feet.

As far as possible, washing a pony should be avoided. It is never good for the animal and may be actively harmful. Especially in winter, there is not much justification for deliberately wetting the animal's skin. As far as removal of dirt and mud are concerned, it is always best to let the coat dry, and then brush it clean. Washing the hair tends to remove some of the natural, healthy oiliness which gives it shine. This spoils the look of the animal.

Occasionally in summer a pony is washed before some special function such as a show, particularly if the animal is white, or has white legs which become stained. The smallest area possible should be wetted, and washed with household soap, or a medicated animal shampoo, and never with a detergent. Great care is necessary to ensure that all the soap is rinsed out. A pony's tail is washed most easily by dipping it into a bucket of warm water, soaping it, and then dipping it again to rinse it.

Once washed, the pony must be dried as rapidly as possible. Start with the sweat scraper if necessary. Follow this by rubbing over with a clean towel or straw, and then putting on a sheet or light blanket and bandages. If the weather is hot and sunny, a pony walked around in the sun will dry off just as well. One harmful effect of washing a pony is chapping of the skin, or mud fever. This is traditionally due to lazy grooms washing the mud off horses' legs instead of waiting for it to dry and then brushing it off. Cracked or greasy heels—soreness in the heels with an accumulation of skin secretion around it—are mainly due to the animal's legs being repeatedly wetted and not dried properly.

The Mane

Routine attention to the pony's mane has already been described. The mane looks neatest if it falls all to the same side of the neck, usually the off side. Repeated brushing helps to make it lie flat, but sometimes this is not enough and the hair continues to grow in all directions. A remedy for this is to wet the mane and then braid it, causing it to lie on the appropriate side, and leaving the braids in overnight. Some ponies do, however, have such naturally bushy manes that it is hard to make them look neat. This is especially likely if the mane has at some time been roached, or cut to only a couple of inches in length.

A mane that is too thick can be thinned by pulling. This is done after the mane has been thoroughly brushed, by taking a few (usually the longest) hairs at a time from underneath, and pulling them out quickly with your fingers, or by winding them around a mane comb. This is continued until the mane is thinned as much as you want. Ponies seldom seem to object to the procedure unless too many hairs are pulled at the same time.

A mane which is too long is also shortened by pulling—never by cutting with scissors, which will spoil its appearance. The long hairs are simply plucked to the required length, usually about three inches, but this is very much a matter of taste. Some owners prefer to let their animal's manes grow very long, and do nothing more than thin it occasionally, if that. However short the rest of the mane is, the forelock should be left long and thick enough to offer some protection from flies in summer.

Hogging a mane is really taking the shortening and thinning processes to its extreme, and means the nearly complete removal of the mane with clippers. This saves grooming time and looks nice on a stocky animal. Hogging is not recommended, however, for ponies kept outdoors, as the mane provides some protection from the weather. Before a mane is hogged, it should be reasonably clean and dry. The sides are dealt with first, then the middle part of the mane. Whether the forelock is left or not is a matter of taste, though its protective value from flies should not be forgotten.

It is common to completely remove a short stretch of a pony's mane about 2 inches in length at the poll, where the bridle's headpiece lies and the mane may get very knotted, and also from 2 to 4 inches at the pony's withers, where the hair may get in the rider's way and become tangled with the reins. These areas require frequent clipping to keep up with any new growth of the hair.

For a special occasion, such as a show, it may be desirable to braid a pony's mane. This should be done with the mane clean and well brushed. You will need a comb, a water brush, a pair of blunt-ended scissors, a reel of thread to match the mane and a blunt, thick needle. Instead of a needle and thread, rubber bands are often used to secure the braids but they do not give such a pleasing finish.

The mane is dampened with the water brush to make it more manageable and divided into about seven separate locks. The first lock is braided tightly to make a short pigtail, a thread being included in the lower part of the braid. The end of the braid is then tied around with the thread to stop it from coming undone. Then the braid is wound up so that it forms a small, tight knob at the root of the hair. It is then secured with the thread, using the needle to draw it through and through, being careful not to jab the pony. The thread is finally tied off and cut short.

The Tail

The tail is normally brushed, just like the mane, from the roots, one lock at a time. The end of the tail is often trimmed off horizontally with a pair of sharp scissors. Many a pony owner has unfortunately produced a pony with a very short tail, because it is all too easy to forget one simple fact. When a pony is moving, the tail is carried considerably higher than when standing still, and this should be allowed for when trimming. It is easier if there are two people. One holds up the pony's tail at more or less the position in which it is carried when moving. The other gathers up the hair in one hand and cuts it straight, usually level with, or about 2 inches below, the animal's hocks. It may improve the appearance if the line of the cut is very slightly upwards, toward the pony's back legs.

Fig. 26. Braiding a pony's mane.
1. The hair is combed and made into a long braid, with the thread incorporated.
2. The end of the braid is secured.
3. The braid is wound up to make a tight knob, and stitched in place, or secured with an elastic.
4. The thread is snipped off, leaving the pony with completely braided mane.

The top of a pony's tail is often very bushy and untidy. This can be remedied by pulling, just like with the mane, thinning out the hairs on the sides and upper part of the dock, and leaving those on the top looking neat and tidy. The pony's tail is brushed first and a very few hairs at a time plucked out quickly from the underside. The use of scissors on the top of a tail will have a disastrous effect on its appearance.

The effect of a tail which is narrow at the top and full below can be enhanced by the use of a tail bandage. The bandage is applied to a brushed and dampened tail. Dampening the

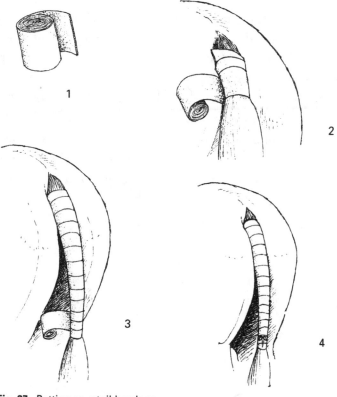

Fig. 27. Putting on a tail bandage.
1. Bandage rolled, with tapes inside.
2. Starting at top of tail.
3. Working downwards.
4. Tapes tied below end of dock.

bandage directly should be avoided, because the bandage may shrink, and hurt the pony's tail. Working from the top of the tail downwards, and securing firmly enough to prevent it from slipping off, though not so tightly that it damages the pony's dock. It should be fastened below the end of the dock. Tying the bandage tightly around the dock itself could cut off the blood supply and lead, conceivably, to the end of the pony's tail dropping off. The tail bandage is removed by grasping it at the top and simply sliding it off the tail, which should, after being bandaged no more than a few hours, be set into the required shape.

Instead of pulling and bandaging a pony's tail into shape, it may also be braided. For this, a tail with plenty of hair at the top of the dock is preferred. It is brushed thoroughly and dampened with a water brush. Starting at the root of the tail, a small lock of hair is taken from each side of the dock, and one from the center. This far up on the tail, the hair is short, and only one crossover of a braid is possible before more hair has to be taken up and braided in, braiding in this fashion down the center of the pony's dock. Lower down, the hair is longer and it is possible to

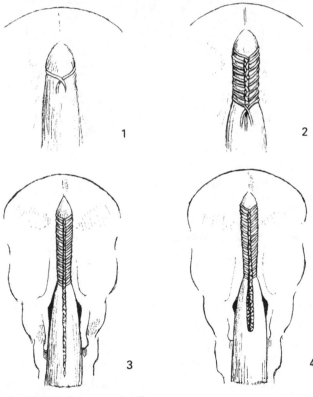

Fig. 28. Braiding a pony's tail.
1. The first cross-over.
2. Working down.
3. With the long "tail."
4. The "tail" is doubled under and sewn in place, to give the finished effect.

make a long central braid which can be doubled under once, and then secured in place (see fig. 28).

Trimming the Pony

Many ponies tend to grow heavy beards, and hair on their fetlocks. This may not look very neat on an otherwise well-turned out animal. A beard of hair between the lower jaws can be removed carefully with scissors, though care is needed to avoid leaving cut marks. Clippers may also be used.

The whiskers on a pony's muzzle and at the eyes are sometimes removed for a smarter look. This is unkind, however, to an animal that gets its food by grazing, as the whiskers are used for sensors to tell how close the nose is to the ground. The hair inside the ears should not be removed, either, unless there is a large enough quantity to look very untidy. Then only enough should be trimmed to provide a neater appearance. The hair is there to keep the insides of the ears warm.

The hair on the pony's fetlocks may also be trimmed or removed and in the summer this is not likely to do any serious harm. In winter, a pony living outdoors should be left with all its hair, and this does not look so untidy. Some ponies grow only a little hair here and this can be removed by plucking. Scissors or clippers can also be used, though care is needed to prevent unsightly marks and unevenness.

When clipping the pony's heels do not forget that there is the little horny ergot at the hindmost point on each fetlock and this is very easy to cut accidentally. The ergot normally requires no attention. Its function, it has been suggested, is to protect the point of the fetlock when the pony's heel sinks so far as to touch the ground, as might happen when landing after a jump, for example. Occasionally, action pictures of steeplechasers or show jumpers show this.

The function of the chestnut, the horny lump on the inside of the pony's legs above the knees and below the hocks, is less easily explained. Generally the chestnuts need little attention, though they grow continually. Sometimes they become large enough to get in the way when the pony is moving, or to be in danger of being torn off. If so, your farrier can be asked to pare them down, or you may be able to peel off some of the outer layers without causing the animal any discomfort.

Chapter Ten

CLIPPING AND CLOTHING

A pony sheds twice a year. This is most noticeable in the spring, when a large quantity of hair is shed, and the short, sleek, summer coat grows in. In the fall, these short hairs are replaced once again by the longer and slightly more greasy ones of the winter coat. This heavy coat keeps the pony warm, and the oil in the coat helps make it waterproof.

When the weather is very cold, a pony's coat actually stands on end. This increases the layer of warm air trapped in the coat, and improves the pony's insulation against the weather. It is the same as a person who puts on an extra sweater to keep warm. This is why it is necessary to brush out any hairs which are stuck together before the animal is turned out into the field, enabling the hair to stand up properly.

The pony can vary the degree to which the coat stands up and, to some extent, control the body's warmth. Even so, if working hard, the pony can get very hot and, because of the heavy coat, sweats a great deal. This can result in a loss of condition and—because the long coat is difficult or impossible to dry quickly—a considerable risk that the animal will become chilled. It is also hard to groom the winter coat thoroughly to make the pony look smart.

Removing the heavy coat with clippers solves these problems, and, if you intend to ride much in winter, it is really a kindness to clip the pony, at least partially. It does mean that, when not working, the pony has no protection from the weather and cannot keep warm. For this reason the pony has to be provided with blankets and other clothing to avoid getting cold while not at work. If clipped, the animal should be housed at night.

Fig. 29. Various styles of clip. (From the top) Fully clipped out, hunter clip, blanket clip, trace clip, small trace clip.

How to Clip a Pony

The summer coat, being fine and short, is never clipped. The winter coat is generally given its first clipping some time in October. It begins to grow again at once, and by January it will require a second clipping; a third may be necessary towards the end of the winter. If so, care should be taken that the summer coat has not begun to come through, as clipping may damage the new growth.

Electric clippers are normally used to clip horses. These can be powered directly from an electrical outlet, the main, or from batteries, or can be rechargeable. Simple hand clippers are available, but are very hard work over a large area of pony. All clippers should have sharp blades, and any hairs accumulating on them should be blown or brushed off at frequent intervals. The blades should also be kept well oiled during clipping.

It requires some skill to clip a horse with no unevenness or clipper marks. Clippers are used in the opposite direction of that in which the hair grows, and with as level a pressure as possible. Few animals object to being clipped, provided it is done quietly and the clipper blades are sharp. If they are blunt they will pull the hair. The animal's coat must be clean and, as far as possible, free of dust and grease. Test for this by running the fingers through the coat against the hairs. This will produce tracks of dander if the coat is dirty. The presence of grit and grease in the coat greatly increases wear on the clipper blades, which are expensive to replace.

The coat has to be dry before clipping, partly because the clippers do not cut damp hair well, and also because of the risk of giving the pony an electric shock. All clippers should be checked for their electrical safety anyway as, understandably, a pony which has once received a shock from the clippers is suspicious about being touched by them again. Some animals seem to have a natural dislike of being clipped, whether or not they have had an unpleasant experience in the past. If gentle but firm handling will not persuade such a pony to tolerate the clippers, it is probably best to send the animal to a professional, along with a suitable warning. In some instances the problem is so bad that it is necessary for the veterinarian to give the pony a tranquilizer before clipping can start.

Styles of Clipping

A pony which has had the whole coat shortened is said to be clipped out. A *hunter clip* involves taking off all the hair except that on the legs, which is left as protection from the briars and thorns found in rough country. The saddle mark is usually left too. This is not done as a protection against saddle sores. If the saddle rubs, it rubs, and a layer of hair will not prevent damage to the pony's back. It is to prevent direct contact of a cold saddle lining with the pony's naked back, which could make the animal buck. Also, if the hair is left long, there are no short, bristly ends of cut coat to stick into the skin, causing irritation and soreness. The saddle mark is usually left by clipping around the pony's own saddle, which ensures that the patch is a good fit. Remember that the long hair of the saddle mark requires drying when the pony comes in sweaty, because chilling of the skin may cause soreness in that area. This may put the pony off his work.

A pony that is completely clipped will require a considerable amount of clothing and attention to its welfare. Such an animal will find it cold if turned out in the paddock for more than a short time on a winter's day, even if provided with a blanket. The pony will have to be stabled most of the time, and groomed and exercised thoroughly every day.

A simpler approach to the problem of a heavy winter coat is to remove it partially, clipping only areas where there is the most sweating, but leaving the rest of the hair. This reduces the amount of clothing the pony needs. The partially clipped pony can live comfortably outside by day wearing a waterproof blanket, either coming into the stable at night or using a well-bedded field shelter.

The most popular partial clip is a *trace clip*. The hair is removed from the belly, front, and up the sides. It may be taken off the lower half of the pony's head and neck as well, though if more than the minimum is removed, correspondingly more clothing is needed. The *blanket clip* is an extension of the trace clip, or a reduction of the hunter clip, depending on which way you look at it. It involves removal of all the hair except that on the legs and an area like that covered by a blanket thrown over the pony's back.

Clothing

Clothing is needed in winter to replace the coat on a clipped pony and, occasionally—such as when the animal is ill—an unclipped pony may need a garment to keep warm, too. The basic item of clothing is the blanket. This should fit loosely around the animal's neck so that the head can be lowered comfortably to eat. However, it should not be so loose that it slips back and chafes at the withers. Rugs are cut so that they allow room for the pony's withers and rump, and are secured by long webbing straps, which are stitched to the material.

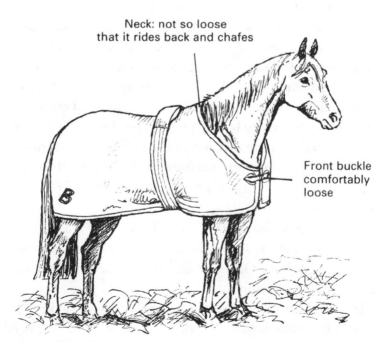

Neck: not so loose
that it rides back and chafes

Front buckle
comfortably
loose

Fig. 30. Proper fit of blanket.

To put on a blanket properly, first the back half of it is folded forward over the front half, and the whole blanket is then gathered up in the right hand. Standing at the pony's near, or left, shoulder, throw the blanket gently over the withers, so that the neck of the blanket is placed forward of its eventual position. This allows it to be pulled back into its proper place, ensuring that all the animal's hair lies flat beneath it. The front buckle of the blanket is secured. It should be buckled more loosely than a girth so that it is not uncomfortable, and it helps if the lower edge can be pulled out a little, so that there is no tightness over the point of the shoulder, which might get rubbed and made bald.

The blanket is correctly positioned when its center seam lies straight along the animal's back. To remove it, simply undo the front buckle, fold the front half back, and sweep it backwards over the pony's tail, leaving the hair smooth and flat. The blanket is then placed out of the way in a dry corner of the stable, preferably somewhere off the ground.

There are a number of different types of blankets, used for different purposes. All are expensive and deserve proper care. This means periodic washing, scrubbing, or even drycleaning to clean the fabric. Any leather straps and buckles should be thoroughly oiled on a regular basis. All blankets should be aired out well and dry before they are put on the pony, because a wet or damp garment is worse than none at all. When blankets are stored, during the summer for example, they are best put away—clean—with mothballs, in a suitable dry cupboard or tack box.

Many blankets are made of quilted nylon and are held in place by straps around the legs or belly. They can easily be washed in a washing machine. On a fine day, the blanket will benefit from an airing in the sunshine.

How do you know whether a pony needs a blanket? A reasonable guideline is that a clipped animal, indoors, will need no rug if the temperature is over 60°F; one blanket if it is between

Fig. 31. A pony clothed in a heavy blanket and leg bandages.

45° and 60°F; a rug and one thick blanket if it is between 30° and 45°F; and a rug and two blankets if the temperature drops below 30°F. A pony which is trace-clipped and stabled usually needs one less blanket than a clipped-out animal.

The temperature used to judge how much clothing a pony needs should be the lowest reached during the night, since that is when the animal will mostly feel the cold. However, the guide given is only an approximate one, and the final decision should depend on whether the animal seems too hot or too cold. The best measure is the temperature of the ears—they should be warm right up to their tips. If they are cold, then an extra blanket may be indicated. Rub the pony's ears gently, too. This seems to have the effect of warming and cheering up the pony. If the pony is too hot, on the other hand, sweat may be apparent, and the damp patches will be obvious. Don't forget that a pony which has just come in from exercise or has recently finished a meal will probably be warm, even though the animal may cool down considerably later on.

Fig. 32. A New Zealand rug.

The New Zealand Rug

Many ponies spend much of their time outside during the winter and for them a New Zealand rug is ideal. Made of stout canvas lined with blanketing, it is waterproof and provides excellent protection from both wind and weather. A New Zealand rug is the same shape as a normal rug, with straps at the front, but also has straps passing around the pony's hind legs, which prevent it being dislodged when the animal rolls. It may have a surcingle as well, though this is not necessary.

A New Zealand rug is too heavy for a pony to wear in the stable, and also too hot. A new rug may be rather uncomfortable when first put on the pony, as the canvas tends to be stiff, and this, plus the different leg straps, may make it necessary to give the pony some reassurance until it becomes used to the garment.

The Cooler

A nice addition to any pony's wardrobe is the cooler which is made of cotton and polyester fabric or of open-weave cotton mesh, or scrim. It is very useful indeed, particularly when the pony comes in hot and sweating, as it will allow the animal to cool off without getting chilled. It covers the horse fully, from head to tail, and down both sides. It also reduces the chances of breaking out into a sweat again later.

The Summer Sheet

This item is made of cotton and/or polyester. It is a very light-weight blanket which is used to keep dust and flies off a clean pony in summer. It does not help to keep the pony warm, but a summer sheet is useful when a pony is being transported to an event, for example.

Since it is so light in weight, the back corners of the sheet are liable to be blown up by the wind. To prevent this, a "fillet string," a light cord of braid matching the binding of the sheet, can be attached to the loops at each corner, so that it passes above the pony's hocks, and under the tail.

Leg Bandages

Bandages are applied to a pony's legs for a number of reasons. Those used to protect wounds and give support (exercise bandages) are described in Chapters 11 and 13. Stable bandages are used to keep the pony's legs warm, and are sometimes used to give protection when the animal is traveling.

Stable bandages are made of wool or synthetic woolen material. They are 7 to 8 feet long, and 4 inches wide, with tapes or Velcro closures sewn at one end. Each bandage is rolled up with tapes or the Velcro end neatly folded in the middle of the roll. It is then applied to the leg, beginning just below the pony's knee or hock and winding the bandage downward around the leg. Bandaging is continued as far down as the coronary band, then the bandage is applied upward again, so that the closure can be secured neatly below the knee, with the knot or Velcro closure on the outside of the cannon bone. A bandage should never be put on tightly, only firmly enough to prevent it from slipping off. Stable bandages are put on the pony to keep the legs warm; they

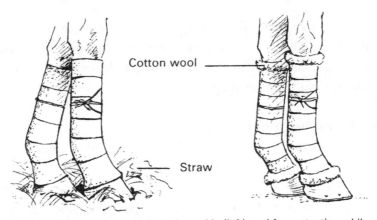

Cotton wool

Straw

Fig. 33. Bandages, for warmth in the stable (left), and for protection while traveling (right).

are particularly comforting to an animal which has had a long, tiring day, is unwell, or is simply feeling the cold during very hard weather.

Bandages may also be put on a pony to prevent its legs being injured when traveling in a trailer. A layer of cotton sheeting or foam rubber can be put under the bandage, since a double layer of bandage fabric alone will not give very much protection. The padding should be extended far enough down to cover the pony's coronary band, since this area is especially prone to injury from the opposite shoe. Even a small cut on the coronary band makes a mark in the wall of the hoof which takes a long time to grow out.

Vetrap, a stretchy synthetic material, is very handy to have for all kinds of bandaging situations, especially in an emergency. However, due to the very springy nature of the material, care must be taken not to apply the bandage too tight, nor to leave it on for too long. It has the added advantage of being able to adhere to itself, which eliminates the need for straps, tapes, or pins.

Knee Boots and Hock Boots

On a valuable pony, in particular, it is a good idea to protect the hocks and knees, since these are more vulnerable areas and may be injured when the pony is traveling. Boots are typically made of thick Neoprene with Velcro closures, or sometimes of a stiff leather or plastic plate set in fabric, with leather straps and buckles, or Velcro fastenings. These should never be fastened too tight. The leather ones are padded with sheepskin or an artificial substitute. The lower strap of a knee boot should be fastened very loosely below the pony's knee, so that the joint can be bent normally. This second strap is there merely to prevent the boot from being turned upwards. The purpose of these boots is to protect the knees from injury and consequent scarring which could occur if the pony were to slip and fall on a hard surface.

The hock boot is similar in pattern to the knee boot. Its main use is to prevent injuries, such as capped hocks, should the pony back into or kick a hard object, like a stable wall or the back of the trailer.

A pony wearing protective leg bandages, knee boots, and hock boots is somewhat restricted in its movement and should not be expected to go faster than a walk. The use of knee boots on horses that are ridden on the road has become popular, though whether they in fact prevent many injuries is debatable.

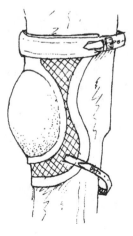 

Fig. 34. Knee boots and hock boots.

Head and Tail Guards

The risk that a pony may throw its head and bang its poll in a stall or, more likely, a trailer, is the explanation for the use of a head guard. This strip of padding, frequently made of Neoprene or foam rubber, is slipped over the head strap of the halter, and should prevent the pony being injured or frightened if its head hits the roof. Alternatively, a poll guard, a cap usually made of leather lined with shock-absorbing felt, can be used.

The pony's tail is prone to damage from rubbing against the back of the horse trailer, particularly if the animal tends—as some do—to lean its rump against the wall to maintain its balance. A tail bandage is frequently used to protect the tail, but a tail guard may be used as well as, or instead of, a bandage. The guard is a piece of soft leather or Neoprene shaped so that it can be wrapped around the tail. It is secured in place by Velcro straps passing around the tail. It need not, and should not, be tight. At its upper end the tail guard has an adjustable leather strap by which it is attached to the roller to prevent its slipping off the tail. Vetrap can also be used for this purpose.

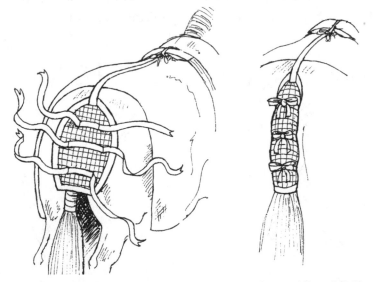

Fig. 35. Putting on a tail guard. Wrapping the guard around the tail (left) and the guard properly applied (right).

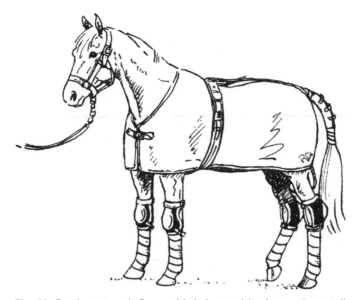

Fig. 36. Ready to travel. Pony with halter and leadrope, sheet, tail bandage, and hock and knee boots.

For a clipped pony traveling in winter, a complete outfit could consist of a blanket, a sheet or two, a cooler or scrim, plus traveling boots (or leg bandages with padding, knee boots, and hock boots), together with a leadrope, halter and headguard, and tail bandage. However, for all but the most delicate animals, a halter and leadrope, a blanket if it is very cold, and perhaps a tail bandage are the main essentials.

Traveling Boots

Nowadays, a wide variety of boots are available, specially designed to prevent injury while traveling. They are usually made of synthetic material which encases the legs from just above or below the knee or hock, down to the coronary band. They are usually fastened with Velcro, and have the advantage of being easy to put on and take off quickly. Their disadvantage is that they have a tendency to slip, so it is important to ensure that they are the correct size for the pony.

Chapter Eleven

THE PONY'S TACK

The most essential elements of a pony's equipment are the bridle and saddle. These sometimes have to be worn for long periods, so attention to their proper fit is very important. The fit is also crucial because you depend on the tack to control the pony. If you ride with weak, rotten, or badly-adjusted tack, your life may be literally hanging by a thread—as may your pony's. On busier roads the chances of a runaway pony getting home in one piece are far from good.

Well-kept and properly fitted saddlery enhances the appearance of the pony and, indirectly, the rider. The tack does not need be expensive, nor even new. Correct fit and good care have a greater influence on the final presentation than the tack's initial cost. Furthermore, a pony loaded with all sorts of gadgets which are not really needed (such as a fluffy sheepskin noseband, a multi-colored

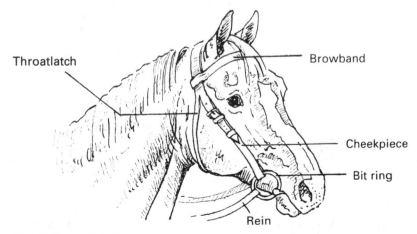

Throatlatch

Browband

Cheekpiece

Bit ring

Rein

Fig. 37. The basic bridle.

saddlecloth, and a set of leg bandages) never looks as neat as an animal turned out wearing only the tack required for the job.

The Bridle

The pony's bridle must keep the bit in place and provide some reins to give the rider contact with the pony's mouth. The basic elements of the bridle are the headpiece, the two cheekpieces, a browband, a pair of reins, and the bit.

The headpiece passes over the pony's poll, and on each side goes through a loop at the ends of the browband. It includes a long thin strap, the throatlatch, which is buckled under the pony's cheek and should always be slack—with about 3 inches or a hand's width to spare—so that the pony is not throttled when arching its neck. The browband is a short strap with a loop at either end, and it is often colorfully decorated. A common mistake is to use a browband so short that the headpiece is pulled tight around the ears. The function of the browband is to prevent the headpiece from slipping back down the neck. There should be room for a couple of fingers between it and the pony's forehead.

On either side of the pony's head, the headpiece buckles to a short cheekpiece, which is attached to the bit by stitching, a buckle, or a stud fastening. The same range of fastenings is avail-

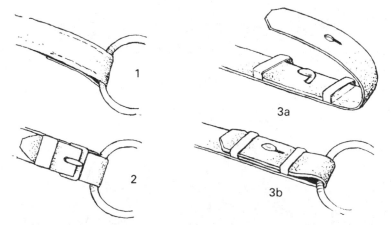

Fig. 38. Cheekpieces and reins are attached to the bit by stitching (1), a buckle (2), or by a stud fastening (3a and 3b).

able for the reins, although studs are usually the neatest, longest lasting, and generally most satisfactory method. The reins themselves may be of ordinary leather, braided leather, leather with leather lacing or rubber hand grips, braided cotton or nylon, or synthetic webbing, as with Continental web reins. Although braided nylon or cotton is unlikely to break, it can cut into the hands, especially if it is thin and the pony tends to pull a lot. Most types of reins are satisfactory, but many people think that there is nothing better than reins of plain, supple leather, and these are probably the best value for the money.

The bit itself can be of several types, although the most common and probably the best bit for a pony is the jointed snaffle. Made of metal (usually stainless steel or nickel), it has a jointed mouthpiece with a ring at each end to which the reins and cheekpieces are attached. The bit should be adjusted so that, with the reins hanging loose, it creates one or two slight wrinkles at the corners of the pony's mouth. If the bit creates more than two wrinkles, then it is probably adjusted too high. It is easy to adjust the bit so that it is too low, however, and this increases the nutcracker action of the jointed mouthpiece. If you open the pony's mouth, the bit should be lying as shown in fig. 39. It should never be so loose that it bangs on the front teeth.

Fig. 39. Proper fitting of the jointed snaffle.

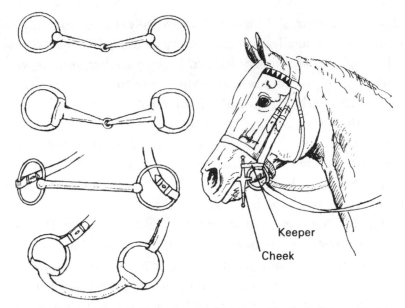

Fig. 40. Types of bit. Left (from the top): jointed snaffle, Eggbutt type, straight snaffle, Half-moon snaffle. Right: Fulmer, or full-cheek, snaffle.

The thicker the mouthpiece, the more comfortable it is for the pony. Some types of snaffle are favored for this reason. It can be confusing, with bits being called by so many different names, but they all belong to one of three or four basic types.

The jointed snaffle family includes the eggbutt snaffle, which has a special junction between the end of the mouthpiece and the bit ring, so that wear does not produce sharp burrs of metal which can hurt the pony's lips. The bradoon is a very simple jointed snaffle designed to be used with a curb bit in a double bridle. The Fulmer or full-cheek snaffle has blunt spikes on either side of the mouthpiece. If you strap the upper end of the spike back to the cheekpiece of the bridle, the bit is stabilized in the animal's mouth. A further modification of the snaffle is the straight snaffle which has rings at either end of a mouthpiece which is a round bar, straight, or slightly curved (a half-moon snaffle). In the latter instance, the inside of the curve should be upwards and backwards so that it fits around the pony's tongue and jaw.

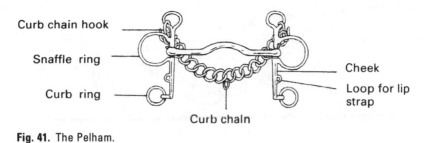

Curb chain hook

Snaffle ring

Curb ring

Cheek

Loop for lip strap

Curb chain

Fig. 41. The Pelham.

The jointed snaffle is generally the most satisfactory bit for a pony. However, some animals perform better or are easier to control in a bit of the Pelham family. These have a mouthpiece which is straight, or has a small hump in the middle (the port) to provide room for the animal's tongue. In the normal Pelham there is a long metal bar, or cheek, at each end of the mouthpiece which acts as a lever and has two metal loops extending from its upper and lower ends. If the rider pulls the rein (the curb rein) attached to the loop at the bottom of the cheek of the bit, pressure is brought to bear on the pony's chin groove by the curb chain passing around the back of the jaw. This may actually be a chain, or a leather strap, or sometimes a chain fitted with a guard of rubber or sheepskin to make the action milder. A curb chain is made to lie flat and not be twisted and it should always be used in that fashion. It is attached to a hook on the bit, and passes through the

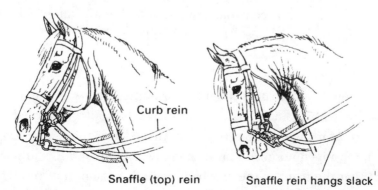

Curb rein

Snaffle (top) rein

Snaffle rein hangs slack

Fig. 42. The principle of the curb. Tension forms as the curb rein tightens, pulling back the cheek, and tightening the curb chain on this double bridle.

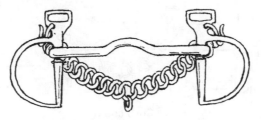

Fig. 43. The Kimberwicke

upper loop on the cheek of the bit (not behind it, where it would pinch the pony's lips), and then behind the jaw to the other side. The spare link in the middle of the curb chain should lie facing outwards; through it passes a narrow lip strap, which buckles on either side to the cheek of the Pelham bit, and keeps the curb chain in place. A lip strap is not strictly necessary on a Pelham, though it is correct to use one.

In addition to the lower (curb) rein, the Pelham has a snaffle rein attached to the upper loop on the cheek of the bit, and this acts like a simple straight bar snaffle. Two pairs of reins may prove to be a bit of a handful, so sometimes short leather straps are buckled from the upper to the lower loops on each side of the bit, and a single pair of reins is used. This same idea is taken further with the Kimberwicke, which has a straight mouthpiece with a port, a curb chain, and a D-shaped ring instead of a cheek, to which a single rein is buckled so that its action is similar to that of a conventional Pelham, though somewhat milder. Most ponies should be able to be controlled in a snaffle, but a Kimberwicke is useful for those that need stronger handling.

Nosebands

The dropped noseband is popular for ponies, and is used in conjunction with a jointed snaffle to improve the control afforded by this bit. Many ponies go very well in this combination. The strap of the dropped noseband buckles below the bit, and it is important that the front of the noseband is high enough not to interfere with the soft part of the animal's nose, where it might impede breathing and cause discomfort. It does not need to be

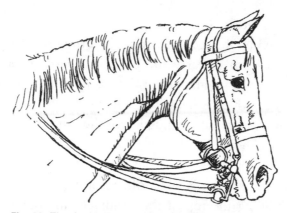

Fig. 44. The double bridle. A bradoon (a jointed snaffle) and a plain curb bit are used together. Rather a mouthful for the pony, and a handful for the rider!

buckled tightly, either, because its effect does not depend primarily on the pony being prevented from opening its mouth.

The cavesson noseband works much like a dropped noseband, though it is buckled above the bit and inside the bridle's cheekpieces. Like the dropped noseband, it is not an essential piece of tack, but is often added through custom, and to improve the bridle's appearance. The cavesson noseband is adjusted so that it is about two fingers' width below the pony's cheekbone, and is buckled loosely enough to admit two fingers comfortably between it and the pony's jaw.

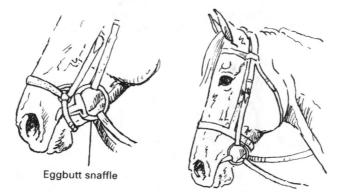

Eggbutt snaffle

Fig. 45. Nosebands. The dropped noseband (left) and the cavesson noseband (right).

Bridling the Pony

Before worrying about how to put the bridle on the pony, the rider should learn to carry the bridle properly when it is off. The buckle in the middle of the reins is placed on the center of the headpiece, which is held over the fingers; this way the bridle does not get tangled up or dragged in the mud, and is ready for putting on the pony.

The reins are put over the head so that the animal can be controlled when the halter is taken off. Standing on the pony's near side and holding the top of the headpiece in your right hand, bring the bit gently against the front teeth with your left. This will make most ponies open their mouths so that you can slip the bit in with your left hand. The headpiece is pulled carefully over the pony's ears, and the mane arranged comfortably, and the throatlatch and noseband buckled up.

Occasionally a pony is stubborn about opening its mouth to receive the bit. Fortunately most animals will open up automatically if you slip your thumb or index finger into the corner of the mouth just behind the front teeth of the lower jaw, though obviously care is necessary to ensure you do not get your fingers mixed up with the teeth! Most difficulties with bridling a pony arise from a previous uncomfortable experience

Fig. 46. Bridling the pony.

with the bit, either by someone shoving it into the mouth roughly, or through rubbing on the lips, gums, or tongue, creating sore or tender areas.

Neckstraps and Martingales

The neckstrap is a useful piece of equipment for any rider, especially young or novice ones, and makes the pony's life a great deal more comfortable. It is fitted low down on the neck, just above the withers and forward of the shoulder. If the rider feels insecure in the saddle—when going over a jump for example—he can hang onto it instead of hurting the pony's mouth by pulling too hard on the reins. A neckstrap can be as simple as a spare stirrup leather buckled around the pony's neck, though neckstraps are available which have a strap which connects to the pony's girth. This prevents the neckstrap from dropping forward around the pony's ears when grazing. Any neckstrap should be fitted a bit loosely around the pony's neck, both for the animal's comfort and so that the rider can take hold of it quickly and easily.

A martingale also provides the rider with a neckstrap, though this is not its primary function. The standing martingale is a type frequently used on ponies. It essentially consists of a strap, buckled at one end to a cavesson noseband (though never to a dropped noseband) and at the other to the pony's girth. It passes between the pony's forelegs, and through a narrow neckstrap. A standing martingale prevents a pony from tossing its head in the air and banging the rider in the face, and stops the animal carrying its head so high that control becomes difficult.

The standing martingale should be adjusted so that it does not come into play until the pony has raised the head above the normal level. As a pony goes over a big fence, or makes an effort to regain balance after slipping or stumbling, the animal may need to stretch out both its head and neck. It is sometimes difficult to

Fig. 47. The standing martingale.

adjust a martingale so that it serves its purpose without restrict-
ing the pony's movement unnecessarily. A running martingale,
which is similar except that it is attached by running rings to
the reins, and not directly to the bridle, does not restrict the animal in the same way, though it is less effective for controlling a
chronic head-tosser. A very useful—and really essential—adjunct
to either type of martingale is a short, thick rubber band, available inexpensively from any tack shop. This is put diagonally
around the slot in the neckstrap through which the martingale
strap passes. It prevents the strap from hanging loose between
the pony's forelegs. This looks untidy and is more uncomfortable
for the animal, which could also get a foot caught in the straps if
allowed to put its head down.

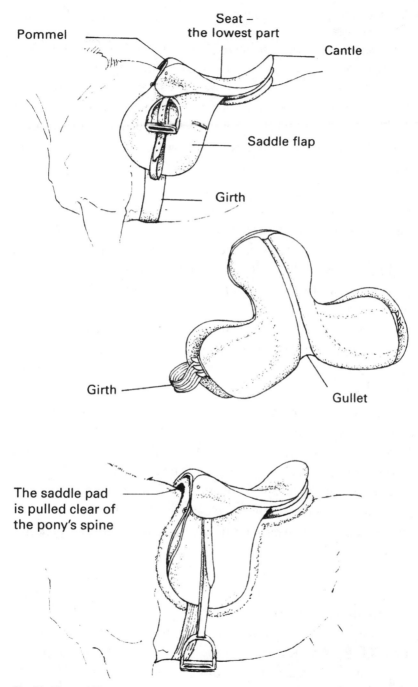

Pommel

Seat –
the lowest part

Cantle

Saddle flap

Girth

Girth

Gullet

The saddle pad
is pulled clear of
the pony's spine

Fig. 48. The saddle.

The Saddle

The saddle is the most expensive item of a pony's tack. It is often the hardest to fit properly, too. It is more comfortable for the rider to sit in a saddle than on the pony's bare back, and the saddle also provides attachment for the stirrups. A most important function of the saddle is to keep the rider's weight off the pony's spine. To do this, it is constructed on a framework, or tree, formerly made of wood but nowadays of metal, which has a central arch over the pony's backbone. The weight is carried on the saddle's padding, or lining, which rests on the thick muscles on either side of the animal's spine.

A saddle that is too wide for the pony will hang on the spine, and nasty sores will result. You should be able to see daylight if you look down the central gullet of a correctly fitted saddle, even when someone is sitting on it.

A saddle can be too narrow as well, in which case it will sit up too high, particularly at the front, and will pinch the pony's withers. Nothing can be done about this fault, except to replace the saddle.

An alternative is to use a saddle pad made of felt, quilted nylon, or sheepskin, or a saddle blanket, which is usually just used with Western saddles. This will sometimes help, as may a wither pad, provided one point is remembered. Every time you saddle a pony, the pad or blanket must be pulled well up into the arch of the saddle so that it clears the pony's spine. If this is not done, the saddle pad can throw more weight onto the pony's backbone and this just makes the situation worse.

The saddle is held on the pony's back by the girth, a broad strap buckled to two or three straps under the saddle flaps. Girths are made of a variety of materials. Flat or folded leather is readily available, but expensive, and has a tendency to chafe unless kept very clean and supple. Cotton, nylon string, or synthetic materials are also used and are less expensive and easy to maintain. Old-fashioned webbing girths are not recommended as they often rot and can break suddenly.

Fig. 49. Saddling up. Stretch each foreleg toward you in turn, to pull any wrinkles of skin from beneath the girth.

The stirrups consist of the irons, the frame carrying the rider's foot, and the leathers, or the straps supporting them. Irons may be of the conventional pattern or the safety type. The latter have a stout rubber band on the outside which comes away should pressure be put on it by the rider being dragged with a foot caught in the stirrup. The leathers, passing through a slot in the top of the iron, are attached to the saddle by a bar which is usually equipped with a metal fastening. This should always be left down so that if the rider is dragged the leather can slide back off the bar.

Sometimes a problem arises when a pony's body is of a very round shape which causes the saddle to continually slip forward. This is prevented by a crupper, a strap which is buckled at one end to a D-ring at the back of the saddle. At the other end it has a loop which passes around the base of the pony's tail. To adjust the crupper properly, the saddle is placed in its correct position and the crupper buckled so that a hand can be passed between its strap and the pony's rump. It should not be too tight, as this would be very uncomfortable for the pony and might cause bucking.

Saddling Up

Before carrying the saddle, run the stirrups up the understraps of their leathers, otherwise they will bang around. The girth is laid over the seat of the saddle, and the whole thing carried over one arm. Put the saddle on the pony's withers, forward of the proper position, then slide it back into place so that the hair underneath is smooth. Saddling and unsaddling are usually done from the near side.

The pony will be more comfortable if you lift each foreleg in turn, and stretch it forward to pull any wrinkles of skin from under the girth. By the time you tighten the girth the pony should have stopped blowing himself out with air, a trick learned by some animals which results in the girth being slack when the rider tries to mount. In fact, the girth never needs to be very tight and you should remember that the best place to test its tightness is at the lowest point of the pony's barrel; slackness down the sides may be deceptive. Finally, hair under the girth is smoothed by running a finger down between the girth and the pony's body. If a folded leather girth is used, its free edge should be to the back, since it could chafe and rub the skin raw if it lies facing forward.

A saddle pad is put on first and in the same way, and drawn back into place so that it is smooth. The saddle is put on top of it. The pad is then pulled up into the saddle arch and the girth is buckled before any straps or tapes which attach the pad to the saddle are fastened. If the pony's tack includes a martingale, it is important to check that the strap to the girth passes in the center between the pony's forelegs, because it may chafe if pulled to one side.

Cleaning Tack

Tack is expensive and deserves good care. The moment it is taken off the pony it should be placed over a suitable fence or door, out of harm's (and the pony's) way. Tack should be cleaned regularly, preferably every time it is used, to remove any salty sweat which damages the leather, and layers of mud and scurf which can accumulate.

It is better to disassemble tack before cleaning. The bit and stirrups are then scrubbed with warm water, dried, and polished. The leather is washed with tepid (not hot) water and, if necessary, saddle soap (never detergent, which spoils the leather) to remove the coating of grease and scurf. It is allowed to dry, then a dressing of saddle soap or neatsfoot oil is rubbed well into the leather. This helps to keep it supple, repels moisture, and preserves the stitching. It is important not to use too much grease or soap and also not to just smear it on over layers of dirt. It is a bad, but very common, practice to just wipe soap over the equipment to give the surface a shine. If you look carefully, you can see the nasty thick coating of a black mixture of soap and scurf and grease and mud and grit; the last two in particular are bad, because they will wear on the surface of the leather and damage the pony's skin.

The girth, if it is made of synthetic material, can be washed in a machine and dried overnight. If time does not permit this, vigorous brushing will remove dried mud and dirt. Webbing girths can only be cleaned by brushing with a dandy brush, and leather ones should be cleaned and oiled like the rest of the equipment, though it is especially important to remove any excess saddle soap from them. This also applies to a leather saddle lining. Other types of lining can only be cleaned with a brush because, if wetted, they are difficult to dry properly. Sheepskin pads and girth guards are cleaned by brushing, although other types of saddle pads can be washed in a machine

The location where tack is stored is important, not only because of the risk of it being stolen, but because air temperature and dampness have a detrimental effect on leather. Ideally, tack should be hung on proper racks in a moderately dry atmosphere, such as that of a centrally heated house or tack room. If it gets too hot, as it would by a fire or furnace, for example, leather can become brittle. Conversely, if kept in a very cold, damp place, it absorbs water and will feel sodden. In a warm, damp atmosphere the leather will often grow large quantities of mold—an indication that it should be kept somewhere else.

While you are cleaning tack you should examine certain places that tend to wear badly. Bits will wear most at the junction of the mouthpiece with the rings in a snaffle bit, or the cheeks in a Pelham, which can cut the pony's mouth. The stitching of all tack usually has a shorter life than the leather, and it is worth remembering that sound leather can always be restitched. Straps tend to give way first at the holes, a good reason for undoing all the buckles of the tack when cleaning it. It helps move the buckle of the cheekpiece down on one side of the headpiece and take it up on the other side to compensate, to transmit the wear to new holes.

Stirrup leathers tend to wear badly at the holes, especially if they are used persistently by one person who would have them set at the same length all the time. Periodically they should go to a saddler to be taken up a few inches at the buckle end. The girth straps on the saddle require examining for wear, which includes checking the stitching at their upper ends. A buckle guard, which is a thin piece of leather with narrow slots to fit the girth straps through, is usually fitted over the girth buckles to prevent their chafing the saddle flap, since holes in the flap are very difficult to repair. With tack, as with so many things, prevention is better than a cure. By watching out for early signs of wear, serious damage can often be avoided, thus prolonging the life of the tack, and possibly preventing a bad fall.

Chapter Twelve

OUTINGS FOR YOUR PONY

Looking after the pony while you are out riding is just as important as attending to the animal's daily needs in field or stable. As far as the outdoor pony is concerned, being ridden may disrupt the daily routine built up around feeding times, regular periods of grazing, visits to the water bucket, and periods of dozing. When ridden only occasionally, some ponies might even feel that this is a bit of an imposition, though most seem to enjoy an excursion into the interesting world outside the field, even though it means that they have to work and may come home tired. This applies more to animals which are kept stabled and may suffer badly from boredom and loneliness especially if there are no other horses in the building.

Exercising the Pony

Ordinary work, for example just going for a ride, is sometimes called exercising to distinguish it from special outings, like pony shows, group rides, and other day-long occasions. These require extra preparation and effort, and are usually more taxing for both the rider and the pony. After an ordinary ride, both should return quite fresh as you are unlikely to be out for more than an hour or so, or to go very far from home.

You may choose to enjoy a daily ride along the roads or trails (hacking) or devote the time to training the pony in the field or paddock (schooling). Or, better yet, a little of both. Most ponies seem to prefer going out for a hack, which is less exhausting for both pony and rider than intensive training. A short period of schooling, say twenty minutes every day, followed by hacking,

Fig. 50. You should observe road signs.

will yield better training results than an occasional marathon schooling session. This is not likely to have a beneficial effect, but just leaves tempers frayed on both sides.

Whenever mounted, a rider should wear a hard hat to protect his or her head should a fall occur. The hat should fit properly, and should also comply with ASTM specifications, and withstand a substantial blow. The chin strap must always be fastened and be adjustable to fit the individual rider, so that it is not loose and cannot possibly come off during a fall. Always wear proper footgear—jodhpur boots or knee-high riding boots, not rubber rainboots which are very likely to get caught in the stirrups in the event of a fall.

A greater incidence of auto traffic in some areas makes riding on the roads less pleasant and more risky. A pony which is frightened of motor vehicles is a dangerous animal, and should probably be sold or traded, regardless of its other virtues. In traffic, keep to the left and always make hand signals to alert drivers to your intentions. Observe road signs just as if you were on a bicycle or in a car. Since a rider is going much more slowly than other traffic you should, whenever possible, ride close by the side of the road and on the shoulder—unless it is a footpath or a mown lawn.

A pony should always be kept under complete control when traveling on a road. The reins should be held short enough to allow you to deal quickly with an emergency. Keep to a walk or steady trot since the road surface is very hard and may also be slippery. Never canter on the road, nor on the shoulder on busier roads. If you are ever uncertain whether you can control a new pony, it is much better to be safe and have someone accompany you on a bicycle or on foot to start with.

Avoid riding at night whenever possible. If you do have to ride in the dark, remember two things. First, the pony is most likely to be frightened by the headlights of cars when their light reflects on such ordinary objects as trees and gates, and momentarily makes them look strange and unfamiliar. This may make the pony shy suddenly and head out into the middle of the road—and possibly into the path of an oncoming car. To prevent this, use your leg and rein together on the same side, to bend the pony's head away from the cause of the fear. This also stops the hindquarters from being swung out into the road. Second, you are in danger because you will be almost invisible to drivers. If you must ride when it is getting dark, wear fluorescent safety clothing with reflective strips on your pony and yourself (such as vests, belts, arm, and fetlock bands). Stirrup lights are also available. In an emergency, tie a white handkerchief to a stirrup or to your pony's tail.

If it is possible to get onto a trail or path where there is no traffic to worry about, then you can really relax. Have consideration for the farmer, and be sure to shut gates, walk quietly past farm animals, and as far as possible keep to the edge of fields sown with crops. If you wish to ride over land where there is no trail, for example in woods or over stubble, it is necessary to find out who owns the land and ask permission before going on it.

Footpaths, it should be remembered, are rights of way only for pedestrians, and ponies may not be ridden along them.

Besides being enjoyable, daily exercise makes both pony and rider fit. An hour's riding a day is the minimum for a stabled pony. It is important that the route be varied each day because the animal can easily become very quickly bored with the same old roads and trails. It takes some time to get a pony fit for really hard work, and the daily exercise should be increased gradually, with a corresponding buildup of the grain ration. When you first began working the pony again after a very long break, an hour of walking with a little slow jogging may be about all that is advisable to avoid stressing the pony too soon. After a couple of weeks the pony will be able to manage longer periods of steady trotting, and, after a month of regular work, should be quite fit.

If you have not been riding the pony regularly for a long time, it will probably be the case that both rider and pony will get fit together. Your own stiffness and soreness will tell you if you have ridden too far, too soon, and it will give you some idea of what the pony is dealing with. It is worth remembering that lameness is often the result of giving an unfit pony too much work, particularly when it is tired. It is at these times that a pony is most likely to stumble and fall. Asking an animal to do more than he is ready for is often a bad policy, as it can cause lameness for a long time.

It is sometimes said that an outdoor pony keeps itself fit simply by wandering around the field. This is only partially true, for meandering around in a paddock is a different matter from the burden of carrying a rider. The back muscles in particular can become weakened if a pony is not ridden for some time. Because of this, it is particularly important for an unfit pony's back to be rested periodically. However, with daily exercise, and probably some extra concentrates in its ration if very hard work is done, a pony kept outdoors should quickly become very fit and ready for considerable exertion.

Special Occasions

Before the daily exercise ride, try to get the pony out of the field early enough to leave it for an hour or so without anything to eat before starting out. This avoids the situation of doing work on a full stomach. The pony needs to be groomed to give a tidy appearance, and the feet will need to be picked out. Before a special outing, you will probably want to do more than that to enhance its looks and performance. Such occasions include pony shows and hunter trials, and organized hunts.

The Day Before

On the day before the event, the pony can be exercised as usual. Extra thorough grooming will be required, and in summer the mane, tail, and legs might require washing if your pony is one of those characters that always looks grimy. After being washed, any wet areas should be scraped with a sweat scraper, and rubbed dry with a clean towel or straw, and bandages and a blanket put on if necessary (see Chapter 9).

It will make life easier for you if the pony can be kept in a stable overnight so that there is no mud to roll in, and it is ready and waiting in the morning. A thick bed will be needed for warmth, and it can be given hay and a feeding of grain. On the day before the event, get your tack cleaned and ready, plus any other equipment which you want to take—or have someone else bring by car—such as a halter and leadrope, blanket or sheets, buckets, and a hay net. Personal clothes should be brushed and laid out too, to avoid a panic the next morning in a search for lost gloves, riding gloves, or a hard hat.

On the morning of the event, the pony will require a feeding early enough to be able to leave at least an hour and a half between finishing the meal and heading out. The pony should be left to eat in peace, so it is probably better to offer the feed, then go away and eat your own breakfast. The next job is grooming. Some gray ponies have an ability to lie on the dirtiest part of their bedding just before a show, so that they are covered with stains (it often seems that they only do this when you particularly want them to be clean and beautiful the next day). Stains will be reduced if the bedding is deep and clean, and if you go out and remove any droppings the last thing at night. The only satisfactory way to remove these stains is to wash them off, wetting only the dirty area and drying it as much as possible with straw and a clean old towel.

The pony's preparation may include braiding the mane and tail (although this is not usually for a hunt). Unfortunately this cannot be done the night before as the braids will become loose and untidy if the pony lies down with them in. But with a little practice, you can become quite good at doing them. Time can also be saved if all the materials, such as elastics, or thread, needles, and scissors are gotten ready the previous day. The pony can be fully groomed, right down to oiled hooves, and left tied up, while you go and change into your own tidy clothes and collect your tack. Then all you have to do is saddle and bridle the pony, and you are ready to go.

Traveling

If you are riding the pony to an event, plenty of time should be allowed so that there is no need to rush. About 4 to 5 miles per hour is a reasonable speed to plan on. If you are not very familiar with the route, a map will be useful. This is not so much to determine the route, which is probably known, but to tell how far you should have gotten by what time. Seven or eight miles is about the maximum distance you can expect to ride to a show or meet. This can vary according to the size and fitness of the pony, and the rider.

Traveling by horse trailer is obviously quicker than riding and allows the pony and rider to arrive clean and fresh. They can also stay later because there is no need for concern about hacking home in the dark.

Many ponies that are transported regularly by trailer seem to have absolutely no objection to the experience. Perhaps they realize that it saves a good deal of walking! Generally the transport vehicle is fitted with stalls, and an example of suitable dimensions would be a length of 6 to 8 feet, a height of 7 to 8 feet and a width of about 2½ feet. These measurements must depend to some extent on whether the pony is large or small.

The pony should be tied up inside the trailer, using a quick-release knot, and a sufficient length of rope for comfort, but not enough for there to be any chance of becoming entangled. A hay net, or hay in a manger if there is one, may help to keep the animal occupied during the journey. If it is a long ride there should also be a stop to give the pony some exercise by walking it on a lead, a drink, and a chance to urinate. Those not used to driving a horse trailer should remember that the animals are traveling standing up, and have to find, and keep, their balance. When starting up, the speed should be kept to a minimum, and driving should always be smooth and steady. A pony that is frightened by a rough ride may refuse to ever go into a trailer again.

A pony that is difficult to load always presents a problem. A professional transporter can often get an animal into a trailer where others might fail. If no such help is available, you will just have to do the best you can. Walking the pony straight in is much more likely to be successful if you are looking straight ahead rather than backwards. A reward given once in the box should make the pony easier to load the next time. For ponies that persistently refuse to go in, a person standing on either side can use a long rope or nylon longe rein drawn around the hindquarters to help encourage the animal to walk up the ramp. This method is often effective, and the person at the pony's head should be prepared for the sudden decision by the pony that it is best to oblige after all, as it may go in with a rush.

If a pony has been difficult to load in the past, doubts about the trailer should be overcome gradually. This can be accomplished with daily feeding inside the trailer. At first you may have to be satisfied with placing the feed just inside the box, and watching the pony stretch its head in to eat, but slowly its confidence will

Fig. 51. At a pony show, do not sit on the pony's back for hours.

increase and you will be able to put the feed right inside. It is important that during this time the floor of the box is well bedded down, so that there is a good foothold. A sprinkling of sand can also be useful for this purpose.

At the Event

You go to pony events to enjoy yourself, and ponies often seem to enjoy these gatherings too. No doubt they make a welcome change from the normal routine, and provide interesting contact with other ponies. Remember that they are naturally herd animals. Do not neglect your pony's welfare during the day. You shouldn't use the pony's back as a grandstand for hours, sitting there chatting with all your friends. Do not ride here and there aimlessly, jumping practice fences over and over again. Ponies cannot be expected to give their very best when it comes time to actually performing when treated like this. By then, they will be tired out and fed up with all the activity.

Whenever you get the chance, get off the pony's back, run the stirrups up the leathers, and loosen the girth. During a long day, every animal should be given a proper rest, the bridle being replaced by a halter and the saddle removed. The pony can then be watered. After a long cool drink (enjoyed more fully without a bit in the mouth) the pony can either be held while grazing, or be tied up in a quiet place well out of range of other ponies to avoid kicking matches. It is kind to provide a hay net to pick at while you are enjoying your own lunch.

Never sit on the back of a pony which is not wearing a bridle. You do not have proper control over even the quietest pony when riding with only a halter. You must resist any temptation to jump on the animal's back on its return from the watering area, for example.

At the End of a Long Day

When the event is over, the pony is probably going to feel as tired as you do. The next job is to get you both home as soon as possible. If returning by trailer, the pony should be loaded only when cool and dry, so it comes off the trailer in the same condition at the other end. If you are riding home, trot back steadily, interspersed with short periods of walking when it may be more comfortable for both of you if you dismount and lead the animal. This stretches your own legs and also eases the pony's back. Once again, you should aim to bring the animal in cool and dry. Leading the pony for the last part of the journey helps with this. Loosen the girth for this last stretch, and move the saddle a bit so that air gets between the lining and the pony's skin. Then the saddle mark should be dry, too, when you get home, and some time spent rubbing the pony down will be saved.

If the weather is good, so that the pony can lie down and rest outside, an animal living outdoors is probably better off put out in the field for the night. Before this, a quick brushing over the saddle and bridle areas will restore circulation and remove sweat marks. This makes the animal more comfortable, though its primary concern will, no doubt, be to have a good roll. Of course, the feet should be picked out clean before the pony is turned into the field, and any braids undone. If the animal has had a particularly tiring day, it might be a good idea to give an extra feeding of grain, even in the summer. This meal should not be a large one, because the combination of an additional large feed with exhaustion provides an ideal setting for colic.

In bad weather and in winter the pony is probably better off being stalled for the night, giving it somewhere comfortable to rest out of the weather. Ponies are like people in feeling the cold more easily when they are tired. A good feeding and hay will be needed, although again not too much feed if the pony is not used to it. Checking on the pony the last thing at night allows you to make sure that it is neither too cold nor too warm. The former, detected by using the animal's ears as a thermometer, can usually be remedied by rubbing the animal down briskly and putting on a blanket.

The following morning, whether the night was spent indoors or out, the pony should be checked over for any little injuries which might not have been spotted in the excitement of the previous day, and also for any lameness. Apart from this, the pony, and probably the rider too, deserve a day's rest.

Chapter Thirteen

VETERINARY CARE

Your goal should be to keep your pony in good health, so that you do not have to spend time, effort, and worry on nursing him during sickness, and he does not have to suffer the discomfort of being ill. Occasionally things do go wrong, however, but you must not try to decide for yourself which of the vast range of equine diseases has struck. This is a job for the veterinarian. It is more important for you to learn how to detect the pony's ill health in the first place, so that you can call in the vet at the right time, preferably early on in the course of an illness. The veterinarian is the expert on the complex subject of animal disease, and if a pony is sick, then the sooner he is seen by a vet, the better.

Deciding whether or not to call in the vet often presents a problem—particularly if you have not kept a pony before. It takes some time to learn to detect at a glance, as an experienced horseman can, whether a pony is well or not. You may be suspicious that all is not right, but you may still be left with a feeling of uncertainty. Unfortunately, there are no hard and fast rules which can be laid down on the subject. It is simply a matter of looking at horses and ponies under all circumstances, so that after a while you know almost by instinct how a fit pony should look, and signs of illness will not be so difficult to detect.

Some signs help to identify the healthy pony. His eyes are bright, and the animal is alert enough to notice anything interesting which appears—such as another horse passing by—or someone bringing food. His coat has an underlying gloss, even though it may be underneath a layer of mud. The horn of his hooves has a slight natural shine, too. His hair should not come out in large amounts, leaving behind bald patches, although he will shed his coat obviously in the spring, and again in the fall. A healthy pony, although scratching itself occasionally, will not rub against trees and posts until areas of skin become thickened and inflamed and bare spots appear.

An unwell pony *is* miserable and *looks* miserable. He stands stiffly, with his head and tail down, and his coat dull and staring because it lacks its natural gloss. His ears are at "half-mast" too, neither pricked forward nor flat back, and they stay in that position. A healthy pony moves his ears continuously to hear all that's going on. Often sick ponies go off their feed, though they usually will continue to drink water. They are also reluctant to move, and may feel very hot or cold, sweating in patches or shivering. In many cases, the first sign of sickness is that the pony becomes listless and will not graze or clean up its grain ration.

In a normal, healthy animal, there is little or no discharge from the nose or eyes, while in some diseases considerable amounts of watery or thick material may be produced. If there is evidence of any puffing or panting, it is often hard to decide whether it is the result of exertion if a pony is rather overweight and unfit, or if it is because there is something wrong with his breathing. Extra weight is just as often a problem with ponies as being too thin, because many pony owners tend to overfeed their animals. They are doing their ponies a disservice, because a fat pony is not necessarily more happy or healthy than a starved pony is, and a reasonable medium is the real goal. Remember that in a pony, the ideal weight should be judged by the condition of the whole body, not just by the size of the belly.

Treatment of Wounds

Ponies, like humans, tend to acquire various cuts and scratches in the course of daily life. Small wounds generally heal satisfactorily, with no more attention than washing the dirt away with clean, warm water, plus a little mild antiseptic. Salt water (one spoon of salt to one pint of warm water) is one of the best natural wound irrigation solutions for flushing out debris and dirt from small cuts and scratches. This salt solution can be put in a hand-held garden sprayer, and kept handy in the stable for flushing and cleaning of such wounds. Avoid very strong applications such as the traditional tincture of iodine, which can often do more harm than good, by damaging the delicate tissue of a healing wound. If something must be put on the wound after cleaning it, the best is an antiseptic ointment of the nongreasy type you would use on yourself. Most small wounds heal perfectly well if they are left uncovered. If there is trouble with the area becoming dirty again, or with flies settling on it, then a clean bandage, loosely applied, may help, as might stabling the pony.

When using bandages to cover wounds, avoid self-clinging, synthetic bandages. It is safer to use a felt bandage, which should not be applied too tightly on the pony's leg. You should always pad underneath bandages with a clean, fresh piece of cotton sheeting to equalize pressure over the pony's leg. Remember that small cuts and wounds may swell underneath bandages, and what was a properly fitted, snug bandage can rapidly become extremely tight during the night. This can cause the skin to die, because it becomes trapped between the swelling tissues of the leg and the bandage itself, and loses its blood supply.

Mild and superficial injuries can usually be dealt with using your own common sense; more serious ones may require the vet's attention. Four factors will help you to decide whether to call the vet in: how deep the wound is; whether it gapes when the pony moves; whether it is causing great discomfort; and whether you are truly worried about it. If the veterinarian is called, do so as soon as is reasonable after the injury has occurred but, if possible, keep calls to normal waking hours, for the vet's sake!

While waiting for the vet to come, an injured pony should be kept quiet. The injury should be left alone unless there is danger of it becoming dirty, in which case cotton sheeting and a clean bandage should be applied. If there is serious bleeding, and especially if this is arterial (when the blood is bright scarlet and comes out in regular pulses), firm application of a thick wad of clean gauze or cotton helps to reduce the flow.

Apart from the wound itself, an additional risk associated with injuries to horses is tetanus, or lockjaw. The second name is particularly appropriate, because an animal with the disease becomes progressively stiffer, with the jaw muscles the first to be affected. Tetanus is excruciatingly painful and, if untreated, is usually fatal. There are two ways in which you can ensure that your pony will not be affected. Arrange for the vet to give him a course of injections to immunize against it before he has a wound. This will give him long-term protection, provided that booster injections are kept up, and it will save worry, since a pony may contract tetanus from a wound so tiny that neither you nor he may notice it. The other preventive measure is required when an unvaccinated pony receives a serious wound. Then a single injection of antitoxin should be given by the vet to give temporary tetanus protection for that wound only.

Worming the Pony
Even the healthy pony requires regular treatment for worms. Every pony has some parasitic worms living internally, and their numbers have to be kept down as the microscopic eggs and larvae in the pony's droppings contaminate the pasture, although they are not dangerous to people or farm animals. If a horse or pony picks them up while grazing, these will develop into more adult worms, which in turn shed more eggs and larvae. Huge numbers of such parasites can build up both on the grass and in the pony, whose health may be seriously affected.

Worms are most harmful to young ponies, those under five years old. Large numbers can make youngsters thin, anemic, and weak, and may cause sudden illness and death. Older ponies are usually more resistant, though they too need regular treatment for worms, otherwise the pasture will become contaminated even if the pony shows no signs of infestation.

Of the different types of worm which inhabit the pony's gut, one of the most unpleasant is the redworm. This is actually dark gray in color, with the adult about an inch in length. The young larvae are microscopic and have a nasty habit (after being swallowed by the pony) of going on a tour around the animal's body. Along the way, the tiny worms do considerable damage. This can lead to recurrent bouts of colic in the pony's later life. It can also cause weakness of internal veins and arteries which can lead to their bursting and the pony literally dropping dead—a good reason for keeping worm numbers to the minimum.

Worming a pony is quite simple, especially using the paste preparations in a preloaded syringe that can be squirted easily into the back of the mouth. Other wormers (anthelmintics) come as powders which can be given by the owner in food (making sure the pony eats it all), or by stomach tube by the vet. Wormers should be varied, as worms can become resistant if one drug is used exclusively. Some newer wormers are highly effective, killing migrating worm larvae, and only need to be given two or three times a year to adults. Older drugs are only active against mature worms, and must be given more frequently (at six to eight week intervals in the summer). Helpful literature is available with these drugs, which can also be bought from vets.

In recent years, one particular type of worm has received increasing attention. This is the tapeworm, which is extremely common in horses' intestines, and was previously thought to do little or no harm. Tapeworms do not actively burrow into the lining of the intestine, but simply absorb leftover nutrients as the food passes along the alimentary tract. It is for this reason that they were thought to be harmless. There is now good evidence that tapeworms can contribute significantly to the incidence of colic in grazing animals.

There is also good evidence that large numbers of tapeworms can cause physical displacement of the bowel, sometimes even telescoping of one piece of bowel into the other. For this reason, more and more veterinarians are now advising routine treatment to get rid of tapeworms. As tapeworms are picked up when out on pasture, the most logical time of year to do this is when the ponies have finished doing most of their active grazing, i.e. the fall. Most normal wormers will not eliminate tapeworms, and the most common practice nowadays is to give double the normal dose of one particular type of wormer containing a substance called pyrantel pamoate. Your veterinarian will be able to advise you on the actual brand names available for the elimination of tapeworms, and at what dose to administer it.

Not strictly worms, but internal parasites nonetheless, are bots. These creatures have a curious life cycle. The bot itself is actually a large maggot which lives in the pony's stomach, seldom doing any serious harm there. When it is mature, usually in the spring, the bot detaches itself from the stomach lining and passes out with the animal's droppings. Subsequently, it develops into a large fly and the female sticks her little yellow eggs firmly to the pony's hair, usually over the front half of the body. When the pony licks its hair, the eggs are taken into its mouth and the whole cycle begins again. Bot eggs can easily be removed from the pony's hair with a bot knife or tweezers, and many worming preparations will also remove bots from the pony's stomach.

A Pony's Dentist

Tooth trouble may interfere with a pony eating properly and digesting his food, and make him thin and "poor." A foal develops a set of temporary milk teeth, just as all mammals do, and these are shed on growing up. When he is adult the pony has permanent teeth, which include a small tush, or canine tooth, and generally all this happens without trouble. Occasionally, a pony may develop a small extra wolf tooth just in front of his cheek teeth, and if this interferes with the bit, it can make a young pony uncomfortable, so that he tosses his head and fights the bit. If this proves to be a problem then the vet should be

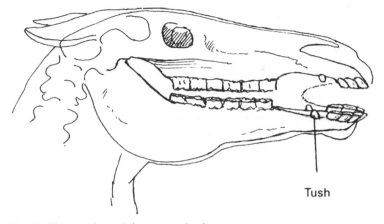

Tush

Fig. 52. The pony's teeth (cutaway view).

asked to come and check the animal's mouth and, if there are any wolf teeth, to remove them.

Most dental problems in ponies arise because the teeth continue to grow throughout the animals' lives. This enables the pony to chew materials as hard as hay and grass without his teeth wearing down too short. It also enables us to tell a pony's age from characteristic effects of growth and wear on his teeth.

If a pony's back teeth do not meet exactly, and many don't, they may grow very rough, with sharp points at their edges so that they are not efficient grinders, and can cut the inside of the pony's mouth. The animal will tend to mess with his food, and never looks really well, despite generous feeding and proper care. The problem is solved by the vet or another specialist rasping down any rough edges at appropriate intervals, usually at least every six months.

Colic

Colic is one of the equine complaints most dreaded by the horse owner. It sounds a simple enough illness—basically a bad stomachache—but it is more serious than that. A pony is very sensitive to digestive upsets, as was stressed earlier (Chapters 7 and 8). The most common cause of colic is worm damage,

Fig. 53. A pony with colic shows signs of pain, such as switching the tail, kicking at the belly, and rolling, as above, or looking sadly at the flank.

though faulty feeding may be one of several other possible causes. All lead to intense abdominal pain, which makes the pony restless and fidgety, with a worried facial expression.

He may pant and sweat and swish his tail, peering occasionally at his flanks. Stamping and kicking at the belly is common,

as is pawing the ground before getting down and rolling franti-
cally. It is common for a pony with colic to keep lying down and
getting up, because he is suffering intense pain.

Most colic is produced by distension of the intestine for one
reason or another. This distension causes pain. The distension
can be of gas, typically following injudicious feeding, or a pony
gorging itself on, for instance, fallen apples. The gas balloons the
intestine, causing pain, and the pain has to be controlled until
the gas passes along the alimentary tract, and escapes from the
rear end. This is known as flatulent colic. The distension may
also be produced by food accumulating within the intestine
because the intestine itself has become displaced. There are
many feet of intestine coiled up in a pony's abdomen, and it is
not uncommon for some of this intestine to become displaced
to an abnormal position. This has an effect similar to tying off
sausages on a string, and prevents the normal ingested material
moving along from stomach to anus. The distension of the
bowel thus produced can cause intense pain, and these bowel
displacements will often require prompt surgical intervention to
save the pony's life.

It was the finding of twisted and displaced intestines in horses
affected with colic which led to the belief that the rolling behavior which colic produces caused the bowel to twist. We now
know that this is not the case: the rolling is the result of the
twisted bowel, not the cause of it. In fact, the reverse may well
be true, and rolling exhibited by a horse with colic may have
some survival value. It is now a common treatment, for some
types of displaced bowel, for the horse to be rolled, under anes-
thesia, from side to side, in order to return the bowel to its normal position. In this way, many cases of what were previously
described as surgical colic can now be cured. Perhaps the first
horses in the wild that evolved the rolling behavior in response
to pain showed increased survival from some of these bowel displacements, causing the behavior pattern to become more wide-
spread in the population.

The final reason why the bowel may become distended is because of impaction of feces. The large colon narrows down significantly as it heads towards the rectum and anus of the pony. The slushy contents of the large bowel gradually have water drawn from them to form the small fecal balls, which are visible within a normal horse dropping. These small balls are produced, one at a time, and accumulate in the rectum, until they are passed as a normal dropping. If the large bowel becomes filled with dense indigestible fiber, it tends to stick like glue. This allows the continuous withdrawal of water over a period of time that is longer than is normal, producing hard, dry feces. This, in turn, produces a blockage in the large colon causing discomfort.

Ponies affected with impaction colic will often lie still and roll onto their backs in order to take the weight of the distended colon off the supporting ligaments which hang from the top of the abdomen. They will try to lie down and stay still for long periods of time. They will usually leave their grain ration, but paradoxically will continue to try to eat hay, making the impaction even more of a problem.

The most common reasons for impaction colic are horses receiving insufficient exercise, and being bedded on straw. This combination leads to boredom, which causes the pony to nibble the straw bedding in between its hay feeds. Straw is basically indigestible and causes the blockage within the large intestines. Impactions require immediate treatment by your veterinarian if further important consequences are to be avoided.

So, if a pony has colic, what to do? There is really no question. Get the vet as soon as possible; time spent trying to treat the animal yourself is valuable time wasted. While waiting for the vet to arrive, it helps if you walk the pony about continuously to prevent it from writhing and rolling on the ground until the vet has arrived. If it is cold, put a rug on the animal. A very deeply bedded stall should also be prepared, preferably with a light for the vet to work by if it is nighttime. When the vet comes, all you can do is follow his instructions to the letter, and hope for the best. Try, with his help, to work out what could have caused the colic, so that it can be prevented in future.

Coughs and Colds

"Coughs and sneezes spread diseases" is true of ponies as well as of people. Ponies suffer from their own version of influenza which is very infectious, spreading either directly, or via contaminated stables, horse trailers, and so on. After contracting the flu, the incubation period is between four days and a week. Then the animal begins to lose his appetite, develops a fever (that is, feels shivery and "hot-and-cold"), and is miserable, with a runny nose. A cough develops, and it is important not to ride a pony if it is coughing. Any exertion during this period increases the risk of permanent damage to the lungs, and a cough which could last for life.

Rest is essential for a pony with influenza. There should also be somewhere warm to sleep at night, as free from dust as possible. It is sensible to ask the vet to visit any pony that has signs of the flu.

Influenza is one of the few viral diseases that can be prevented in the horse by vaccination. The vaccine is given in two doses, a month apart initially, and then every six months to a year subsequently. Although the manufacturers recommend annual boosting only, most people have come to realize that protection from the vaccine is unlikely to last longer than six to eight months. Vaccination every six months will prevent severe symptoms from arising if your pony contracts influenza, and is well worth considering.

Vaccination does not prevent infection of your pony by other viruses, such as the rhinoviruses. Rhinovirus causes the common cold in humans, and a similar virus is responsible for a similar syndrome in horses and ponies. No vaccination is yet possible against rhinoviruses in any species, because these viruses have a habit of changing rapidly in a very short period of time. By the time a vaccine is developed, the virus has already evolved into a new form, for which the original vaccine would not give protection. Basic nursing care and a short vacation are the only answers once a pony becomes infected.

Another common cause of coughing in ponies was formerly called heaves, from the intense effort such animals have to make to breathe. A so-called "heaves line," on the chest wall, is due to abnormal enlargement of breathing muscles. This is not infectious, but is due to an allergy which certain ponies have to mold spores in hay and bedding. It is now more commonly known as Chronic Obstructive Pulmonary Disease (COPD) because the allergy causes chronic lung damage. Horses with this complaint have a harsh dry cough, which is often heard in the stable or at the beginning of a ride, and no nasal discharge. The airway obstruction can be severe, and the animal may be very wheezy.

Similar to human asthma, this allergy cannot be cured, but can be prevented. Ponies with this problem improve markedly if turned out all the time. If stabled, hay and straw should be avoided where possible. Fresh shavings or shredded newspaper bedding are best, and a diet of pelleted feed, formulated to give a complete ration, may be provided. Alternatively, soaking hay, in a hay net, in water for five minutes prevents the spores from becoming airborne.

There are drugs available that will help reduce the severity of symptoms when your pony contacts allergy-triggering dust particles, some of which can be incorporated into the pony's feed. There is also an injection available for use by your veterinarian in the face of any emergency asthmatic attacks your pony may suffer. Besides these drugs, which control the severity of the allergic respiratory disease, there is a range of other drugs, not actually licensed for use in the horse, but derived from drugs used in human medicine, which can be administered in aerosol form via a face mask. This is known as nebulization. Some of these drugs are designed to prevent the allergic reaction actually taking place when the pony is unavoidably exposed to dust challenges. For instance, a pony that is maintained dust free could be treated by an anti-allergy nebulization prior to visiting a show where other ponies may be using dusty hay which cannot be avoided. If your pony is known to suffer from COPD, then it is worth discussing all the possible alternatives for treatment and control with your veterinarian.

The respiratory infection known as strangles is transmitted by contact with other animals which have the disease, or equipment and buildings they have touched. A pony with strangles looks, and no doubt feels, ill, with a fever and no appetite. Characteristic swellings, which sometimes interfere with breathing, develop on either side of the animal's throat, and a nasty white discharge runs from his nose.

Prompt treatment from the vet is important, although with modern drugs it is not the killing disease it once was. Careful nursing is also necessary, and the pony will appreciate a warm stable with a thick bed. Blankets and stable bandages may also be needed to prevent him from getting cold. Wash away dried discharge from his eyes and nose with warm water, and dry the area afterwards with a soft towel. Because strangles is very infectious, the pony should be isolated from other horses, and grooming tools, blankets, and other stable equipment—which can carry the infection—should be soaked in disinfectant and washed.

Fig. 54. A pony with strangles looks ill, and has no appetite.

When the pony has recovered, the bedding should be burnt and the stable walls also cleaned with disinfectant. Your own hands and clothes can also carry infection so it is a good idea to keep an old, washable coat to wear when you are dealing with an infected pony, and your hands should be washed thoroughly when you have finished.

The strangles organism can survive for a long period of time on woodwork, fences, etc. These usually cannot be disinfected if the pony has been out in a field prior to his diagnosis. For this reason, it is a good idea to treat your premises as infected for at least a month after the last clinical signs have been shown by any horse on the property.

Skin Disease
Ponies, especially those in poor condition, are occasionally infested with lice. These active little creatures, brown and about one-tenth of an inch long, are most obvious in the mane and tail. They cause itching so that the pony scratches, and may become bald and sore. A wide range of insecticidal drugs is available to remove lice, which are especially found in winter.

The vet should also be asked about the rarer condition known as sweet itch, which is an irritation shown by thickening, baldness, and inflammation of skin at the bases of mane and tail. No parasites are visible, and the small number of ponies which are affected only suffer from sweet itch during the summer months. The disease is caused by abnormal sensitivity to the bites of certain midges. It usually disappears if the pony is stabled during the early morning and from late afternoon onwards when the midges are around. The stable must be protected from the possibility of midges following the horse into it. This can be achieved by installing metal door and window grills, and if possible fitting a conventional mosquito net on the outside.

Warts are occasionally a problem with young animals, though true warts seldom affect a pony over five years old. They develop mainly on the pony's muzzle, often in a large, unsightly crop, but within three months they usually disappear suddenly.

Saddle sores are not uncommon, arising mainly when ponies have to wear ill-fitting tack. The area of skin which is rubbed become sore and thickened, and may be quite painful. The first thing to do is to stop riding the pony until the tack can be modified so that it does not chafe an already sore spot. Treatment with a mild antiseptic ointment may help the sore to heal more quickly. The most important treatment is usually to find a saddle which fits the pony properly. The areas covered by the saddle and girth should be checked regularly and kept as free as possible of mud and sweat. A nasty saddle sore may require the attention of the vet.

Ponies that are out all the time in wet weather may develop a condition known as rain rot. A bacterial infection forms pus under little tufts of hairs on the back. A similar infection on wet, dirty legs is often called mud fever. Removing the scabs with antibacterial shampoo is usually sufficient to treat rain rot. A soothing ointment will also help mud fever. If the leg swells up, the vet must be called to give antibiotic injections. Soothing ointment is also helpful for cracked heels which are also a problem in wet winter weather.

Ringworm is also sometimes found on ponies' skin. Bald, non-itchy patches appear, often beginning under the girth. It responds to antifungal treatment, but is very infectious, and care must be taken to keep infected tack or grooming equipment away from other ponies.

Azoturia, Monday-morning disease, or tying-up—these names, in common usage, all refer to a disease which is becoming increasingly common in ponies, the technical name for which is exertional rhabdomyolysis. This poorly understood disease produces very painful cramping of the muscles of the hindquarters, and the back of the thighs, which develops as exercise progresses. The pony becomes increasingly unwilling to go forward and will often eventually refuse altogether. Once he stands still, he will scrape the ground, and may sweat and tremble because of the severe pain experienced in the muscles. In extreme cases, the pony may even collapse, or try to lie down and roll as if suffering from colic.

Although most cases of tying-up are relatively straightforward to deal with, in its most severe form the condition can be life-threatening, and is always a cause for concern. Veterinary attention should be sought if the pony is showing extreme pain or unwillingness to move.

When ponies are affected with this disease, the muscles of the hindquarters and along the back of the thighs become hard to the touch and the pony will show a marked pain response if the muscles are prodded. It is probably unwise to force the pony to move, but in extreme cases, such as if the episode happens during a ride, then it is permissible to walk slowly home. If he refuses, then help should be sought and a trailer brought to transport the pony home. A veterinarian will probably want to administer a painkilling drug, and may even suggest intravenous fluids in severe cases.

The causes for this condition are not well understood. The incidence seems to have increased with the growing popularity of Arabs and Arab crossbred ponies, and the tendency to over-feed and underwork pony breeds. While the causes of an individual attack are not well understood, the attacks almost always happen because of a change in the exercise regime of the pony. Tying-up appears to be a problem related to the storage of excess energy by the pony, usually because of a combination of over-feeding and irregular exercise. Although there are no solid rules to prevent all cases of this affliction, the following guidelines will help in almost all cases:

1. Try to ensure that your pony receives the same amount of exercise each day; the pony most at risk is the "weekend pony," which receives scant attention during the

week but, is tacked up and ridden hard on Saturday and Sunday.

2. Try to ensure that your pony spends the smallest number of hours possible in the stable during the day, and is turned out, even if only in a small paddock, when possible.

3. Avoid overfeeding. As discussed in the nutrition chapter of this book, most ponies really only need hay, grass, and water to survive. While the administration of a multivitamin/mineral lick or supplement would be an ideal complement, excessive feeding of high-energy feeds, such as oats, corn, or pelleted concentrates, are contraindicated unless the pony is doing sufficient hard work to need this fuel. Far more problems are caused nowadays by over-feeding of ponies than by underfeeding them.

When you are bringing a pony up to full work, with a view to competing, always try to *follow* your exercise program with feed, rather than feeding ahead of it. In other words, feed your pony for trotting by feeding him as if out of work. When he starts to canter, feed him with sufficient food to trot only. Only when you are ready for full work, step up his feeding regime to a full complement of high-energy feeds.

Monday-morning disease received its name in times gone by because of the tendency of working plow-horses to develop the syndrome, having had a day off on Sunday. If your pony is prone to tying-up, then don't give him a day off!

The Pony's Sex Life

Ponies, like horses, breed during only part of the year. A mare comes into season and is receptive to the stallion for four to six days in every twenty-one. While she is in season, the mare may be more flighty than usual, and show an unusual interest in other ponies. The first "season" of the year is usually sometime in March, and then continuing regularly until September, though individual animals differ greatly from one another.

Mares breed until they are quite old, and any extra risks for an elderly animal having a foal do not appear to be very great. The mare is sent to the stallion to be mated, or covered, for which the owner usually charges a stud fee. He may also ask that the mare be swabbed by the veterinary surgeon to check that she has no infection which she could pass on to the stallion. The gestation period, or the period between mating and foaling, is about 336 days, and the mare can be tested by the vet to see if she is in fact pregnant. If she is, she should not be worked later than about six months before she is due to foal, and then should be fed well.

A novice pony owner would probably be well advised to send the mare to a stud farm, where foaling can be supervised by someone experienced. If the mare is to foal at home, it is generally best to let her foal on her own in a clean paddock if the weather is good, or a large, well-bedded stall if it is bad. The less interference the better during the actual foaling, which usually happens very quickly. Most foals are on their feet and sucking within 2 to 3 hours of birth. The all-too-common recommendations for the pony owner to rush in and sever the foal's umbilical cord are quite wrong. It is via this cord, actually a vein, that the foal receives a large transfusion of blood; it will break in due course, and is best left alone.

A filly (female) foal is allowed to grow up without further veterinary attention, apart from regular worming and vaccination against tetanus and flu. A colt foal will require castration unless he is to be kept for breeding. An uncastrated pony, that is a stallion, tends to be difficult to control and unsafe for normal riding. A colt can be castrated either as a foal, between about fifteen and twenty-four weeks of age, or when he is between a year and eighteen months old. The operation is performed by the vet.

Male horses that have one or both testicles retained in the abdomen are unable to be castrated in the normal way. They are normally infertile but retain some of the sexual ideas of the stallion. They tend to be even more unreliable and bad tempered than "entires" (stallions), and can be very dangerous. By means of a fairly major surgical operation, many of these animals can be made into proper geldings, and then they behave as such.

It is a moot point whether a gelding is preferable to a mare for general riding and driving, and which one you choose is probably primarily a matter of personal opinion. There appears to be little basic difference in temperament, strength, or tendency toward disease, although a gelding which has been allowed to grow up to two years or more as a stallion and then castrated will tend to be a little larger and stronger than a mare of the same parentage. Some people maintain that because of her periodic seasons a mare is less reliable than a gelding for riding; and particularly for competitions, where it is important that she should always give her best, this could be a disadvantage. On the other hand, it is suggested by some that a mare is more responsive as a pet. A gelding has a disadvantage in that if he becomes lame and chronically unfit for riding, his useful life is then at an end, while a mare may still be used for breeding, provided of course that other circumstances—such as time, skill, and suitable accommodation—are also available. For most people selecting a pony for themselves, the decision about whether it should be mare or gelding becomes a minor one compared with whether the animal meets other requirements.

Chapter Fourteen

THE FEET AND LEGS

"No foot, no horse" is an old saying. Things haven't changed—a lame pony is still a useless pony. The pony's legs and feet have to carry a lot of weight, considering how small the hooves are, and how slender even the coarsest of equine legs are compared with the size of the whole animal. This increases the speed and agility of the pony, but means that the feet and legs are highly stressed. However, they are surprisingly tough, and ponies in their natural state seldom suffer from lameness.

The situation changes, however, when we "civilize" the pony. We expect it to work on a variety of different surfaces, for long periods, so that the pony may get tired and clumsy, and at faster speeds than those at which a wild animal would normally travel. The tame pony also has the extra weight of a rider. In addition to all this we expect the pony to work on hard roads, so, to protect the horn of the hooves, we nail iron shoes to the feet. These

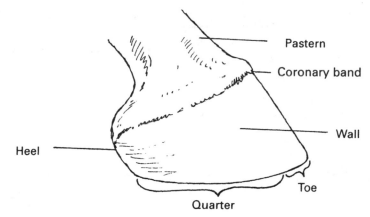

Fig. 55. The hoof.

are bound to have some effect on the natural functioning of the hoof. How great the effect is depends on how well the shoeing is done, for the aim of a good farrier is to make the shoe interfere with nature as little as possible.

The Hoof Itself

The hoof which you see when the pony's hoof is on the ground, is actually the wall of the hoof, the outer shell of tough, horny material. This is similar to, but much stronger than, a human finger or toenail. The wall grows downward continually from the top of the hoof, the region where hair gives way to the fleshy coronary band. The front part of the wall of the hoof is called the toe, the side parts the quarters, and the hind part of the wall is the heel.

The outer layers of the wall of the hoof are insensitive, so that they can be trimmed and have nails driven through them without causing the pony pain. On the inner side, however, the horn of the wall interleaves with about five hundred vertical folds of sensitive tissue, the laminae. These nourish the wall and attach it firmly to the structures inside the hoof. A nail driven too deeply will penetrate this layer and be felt by the pony. This is likely to lead to the accumulation of pus in the area which, in the con-

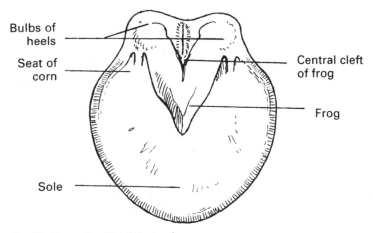

Fig. 56. The underside of the hoof.

fined space of the hoof, is very painful. A pony unfortunate enough to have suffered from this is said to have been pricked, and will usually require quite lengthy treatment from the vet and a long rest before being fit enough for work again.

The outer surface of the wall is shiny. This is due to a very thin layer of an almost varnishlike waterproof material produced by the coronary band. It is very important because it prevents the horn of the wall from drying out, which would make it brittle and inflexible. Removing this waterproof layer by rasping any but the very bottom part of the wall during shoeing is therefore very damaging to the hoof.

If you pick up the pony's hoof, you will see that most of the under-surface is of a slightly flaky-looking horn. This is the sole, which also grows continuously, though it is kept to its proper thickness by the flakes of horn falling off. This happens whether or not the pony is shod. The sole should never be pared, and none but the very loose flakes removed. It is this layer of horn which protects the pony's foot when it treads on, for example, a stone, just as the skin of the sole of your own foot gives protection if you walk barefoot over pebbles.

In the middle of the underside of the hoof is a V-shaped piece of more leathery horn. This is the frog, which is softer and more sensitive to pressure than the horn of the sole or wall. The frog has several functions. First, being sensitive, it lets the pony know whether the hoof has actually touched the ground, as the heel normally hits the ground a fraction before the toe.

Second, it acts as an antislip device—and does this better than almost any man-made one.

Third, the frog is most important in reducing concussion, because directly beneath it lies the digital cushion, a pad of fatty fibrous tissue which acts as a shock absorber. This pad is responsible for the last function of the frog, which is to pump blood around the foot. Whenever the pony puts weight on the foot (provided the frog touches the ground), the digital cushion is squeezed and, like a sponge, forces blood out through the veins

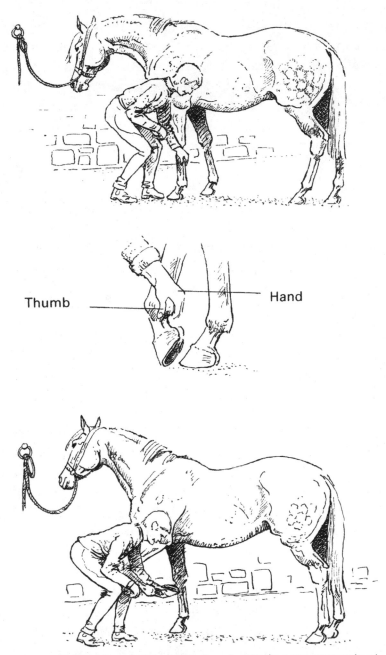

Thumb ——————— Hand

Fig. 57. Picking up a pony's foot. Standing close to the pony, run your hand down its leg (top). As you press gently on the back of the fetlock, the pony will the lift its foot. Hold the foot firmly. A pony that is reluctant to lift the foot can probably be encouraged if you press your finger and thumb on either side of the tendons just above the fetlock.

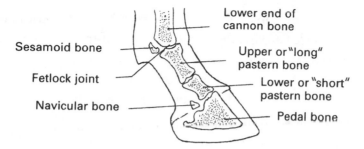

Fig. 58. The bones of the foot.

of the foot. This last function is very important, since the foot is some distance from the pony's heart and circulation may be poor.

It is noticeable that many ponies, if made to stand still for very long periods, will develop slightly filled or swollen legs. This happens because the circulation to the feet and legs is not being helped by pumping of the digital cushion. The filling usually disappears when the animal begins to walk around.

Inside the hoof is, literally, the "end of the pony's leg," the small bones of the lower part of the limb. These are jointed together, and include the relatively large pedal bone and the navicular bone. Like other bones, these can suffer fractures ranging in severity from complete shattering, to a small crack or chip. The joints between the bones may also be injured, with consequent inflammation, pain, and lameness. Whenever the pony puts weight on the foot, there is movement of these bones, as well as of the digital cushion and the wall of the hoof, which expands very slightly.

Shoeing the Pony
The wall of the pony's hoof grows downwards at the rate of about ⅜ of an inch a month. It takes between 4 and 12 months for a piece of horn to grow from the coronary band to the ground surface. Consequently, an injury high on the wall will take some time to grow out, just like damage to your own fingernail. But even though the pony's hoof grows constantly, this will not keep up with the wear that results from trotting on surfaced roads, or even hard-baked or rocky earth. To prevent the horn from being worn back

until the pony is sore, a shoe of iron or steel, or very occasionally plastic, is nailed around the ground surface of the wall. The nails are driven into the wall at an angle, so that they emerge a little way up it, and can be cut off to leave little hooks, or clenches.

The shoe gives such good protection that the hoof grows without being worn away at all. If shoes are left on for more than four to six weeks, serious distortion of the feet can occur. This is why a farrier should be asked to attend to a pony every four to six weeks to trim them. This applies whether shoes are worn or not. The hooves may be reshod with the old shoes, or with new ones. A pony without shoes will also require monthly paring of the feet, especially if confined in a field, because the hooves will not be worn sufficiently to keep them in good shape.

The Farrier's Work

Watch the farrier at work—you will be seeing a highly skilled craftsman, trained over many years, doing a difficult and exacting task. In shoeing a pony, the first job is to remove the old shoes. The farrier knocks up the clenches on the wall of the foot, so that he can lever off the shoe with big pincers. You will notice how the special leather apron he wears gives protection when he rests the pony's foot on his knee for this job.

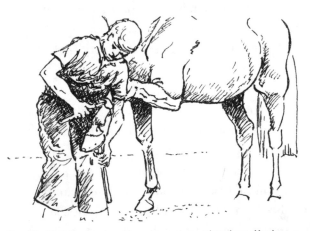

Fig. 59. The farrier tamping down new clenches. He has a special leather apron.

Next, he pares the foot to remove the surplus growth of horn. A special, very sharp, knife is used for this; and a rasp—a coarse file—for reducing the part of the wall which is in contact with the shoe (or the ground, in an unshod pony). This is called the bearing surface, and is rasped to the proper length so that it is completely level. If a pony is to be left unshod, no more is done.

Originally, shoes were made by hand, using the forge to heat them, and a hammer and anvil to shape them. Now, most farriers buy shoes which are ready-made and have nail holes stamped in them, though they still need to be individually fitted to each hoof. In hot shoeing, the shoe is heated so that it is quite malleable and any alterations are made then. A more exact fit can be obtained this way. Cold shoeing is done without the help of the forge, and a good fit is harder to achieve because the cold metal is so much more difficult to work. Hot shoeing is therefore preferred if available, although as farriers become fewer there may be little choice in the matter.

The shoe is fitted approximately to the pony's hoof before it is burnt on; that is, the hot shoe is held in place on the hoof. Despite the searing and the clouds of acrid smoke, few ponies object to this procedure because they cannot feel the heat unless the hoof has been very badly pared. While the hot shoe is held to the hoof, any slight discrepancies in fit become obvious and slight alterations can be made. The shoe should always be made to fit the hoof, but it tends inevitably to be the other way around with cold shoeing.

Fig. 60. The shoe, showing nail holes and toe clip.

Next, the shoe is cooled and the ends of heels filed smooth. Then it is nailed on with horseshoe nails of special, high quality, metal. The number of nails per shoe is kept to a minimum, which depends on the size of the foot, five, six or seven being enough for most ponies. The nails are directed through the wall, and guided accurately by sound, feel, and skill. The points are twisted off and the clenches finished neatly so that they look like small squares of metal in the horn of the wall.

A shoe is more than just a simple semicircle of iron. Most shoes have a small clip of metal turned up at the toe, or on hind shoes, two quarter clips, one on each side of the toe. The clips help to keep the shoe in position and prevent it from being dragged backward. The shoe also has a groove, known as a fuller, running along the ground surface, which helps to give a good grip. Caulks were, and still are occasionally, used to improve the foothold afforded by a shoe. They are made by simply turning under the metal at the heel to make a small step. More often used now are studs of various types, many of which have specially hardened cores to prevent them wearing right off. These may be of the variety which is knocked into the heel of the shoe by the farrier and which stay in place throughout the life of the shoe, or they may screw into a special threaded hole. This second type, often called screws, are more frequently used for ponies competing in jumping and other events where they will not be required to go on the road. Then a larger stud can be used, as it sinks into the soft ground.

The stud is screwed in, usually on the outer heel of each foot, before the competition. The hole in the shoe is normally filled with a plug to prevent it from accumulating dirt. This is removed and the thread cleaned with a tap before the stud is screwed in with a wrench. After the event the studs are removed and the plug replaced.

Another antislip device, not used so much nowadays, are frost nails. These are special horseshoe nails with pointed heads which were put in place of the ordinary flatheaded nails when the roads became icy and slippery. They were commonly used for working animals which had to go out regardless of the weather. They are very seldom used on modern ponies because, if the roads are icy, few people would consider riding for pleasure. Incidentally, if you do wish to ride in snow, the danger is that the snow balls into big icy lumps in the pony's feet. This is prevented by liberally smearing thick grease or petroleum jelly over the sole periodically during the ride.

Against Shoeing

The aspect of having a pony shod which no one likes is its cost, and the attention of a skilled farrier can be expensive. Another problem avoided with the unshod pony is that of casting or losing, a shoe, so that the animal is walking unevenly on the three remaining shoes. Even worse is to have one hanging by a single nail, as the shoe could swing around and injure the opposite leg. Loose shoes make a characteristic rattling or clicking sound as the pony goes along the road. They are usually the result of leaving too long an interval between visits to the farrier, and are generally the fault of the owner. The tendency of the clenches to rise when the shoes have been on too long should be a useful warning.

If shoeing is not done expertly, permanent damage to the hoof may result. If the pony is shod so that the frog never touches the ground, even on grass (when the shoe sinks in), the anticoncussion and pumping actions of the digital cushion are largely prevented. In a pony which is regularly and properly shod, the frog is noticeably well-developed and broad at the heels. This indicates that the blood supply to the foot is kept moving every time the hoof is put on the ground. If this does not happen then there is stagnation of the blood supply, and the whole foot suffers. It has been suggested that this can predispose the hoof to a number of different types of lameness. If a pony is lame and avoids putting weight on one foot for a long time, that hoof becomes narrow, boxy, and contracted, with a small wizened frog. The cause is insufficient weight being applied to the digital cushion to make it compress properly.

In the unshod pony the problem of lack of frog pressure does not arise because the frog is automatically in contact with the ground. Nor does it arise in an animal shod with grass tips. These are effectively the front half of a normal shoe, and are used to prevent the toe of the hoof from splitting. Ponies doing only a little road work are sometimes shod in this manner. Unfortunately, these, like conventional shoes, need removing every four to six weeks, representing no great savings. Money can be saved by not having a pony shod, since it is much cheaper to only have the feet trimmed every six weeks or so. Many animals which are ridden infrequently, or very slowly on just grass, do not require shoeing, and are probably better off without it.

Some injuries may occur during shoeing, though these are uncommon at the hand of a skilled farrier. The prick (or nail driven into the sensitive part of the foot) has already been mentioned. Occasionally a shoe may be put on so that it presses on the sole, with bruising of sensitive underlying tissues as a result. Corns or bruises may develop if the shoe's heel begins to rub there, often because it moves with growth of the hoof. This injury is most often the result of leaving shoes on too long.

Lameness

Lameness is any unevenness of gait exhibited most frequently by a pony limping while trying to avoid putting too much weight on a painful leg or foot. It is not possible to miss really obvious lameness, because the pony will hobble and be reluctant to move, often holding up the affected limb. Mild lameness is not as easy to spot. Foreleg lameness is the more common, since the front legs bear greater weight and are more likely to be injured. To check for this, trot the pony towards you without a rider and with the leadrope slack, on a hard, flat surface (remember that roads have a curve to them). If lame, the pony will probably show it by nodding the head at every other stride. The head comes

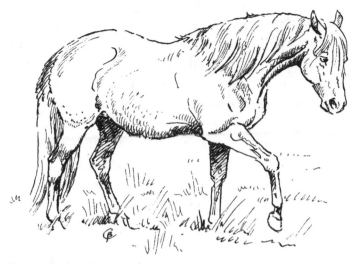

Fig. 61. Obvious lameness is easy to spot.

down as the sound (unaffected) leg comes to the ground. The pony tries to avoid putting too much weight on the hurt foot. Hind leg lameness is not easy to detect, but if the pony is trotted away, you will notice that the hindquarters move unevenly.

Finding the seat or cause of lameness is often very difficult. The vet should be consulted for help and advice, otherwise the lameness may be attributed to the wrong cause and the pony rested pointlessly, possibly for months. Often the injured area can be detected by swelling, heat, and pain in the region, which is particularly noticeable if the lame leg is compared with the opposite sound one. Not all lameness originates below the knee and hock, though much of it does. Injuries to the elbow, stifle, shoulder, hip, and spine may be responsible, and should not be forgotten.

Riding a lame pony will only make it worse. Rest is therefore most important. With many mild strains and sprains, a few days' rest, and repeated application of cold water from a slowly trickling hose, may be enough to effect a cure. If the trouble is more persistent, the vet should be consulted. If it is suspected that the trouble is in the foot, then have the pony's shoes removed before the vet comes, to save time and visits.

Lameness may arise for a variety of reasons and in many different areas. Shoeing injuries have already been mentioned, and these are generally mild. A prick which develops into a large abscess in the hoof can, however, do permanent damage and put a pony out of work for a very long time. Lameness caused by neglect, such as soreness due to cracked heels and mud fever, is usually temporary, provided it is treated. So is thrush, where the frog becomes foul-smelling and oozy. This is usually the result of the pony standing for long periods on dirty, wet bedding, or from not having the feet picked out regularly. The frog becomes inflamed and sore, and the pony is understandably reluctant to work well. Mild cases are simply treated by daily application of Kopertox or a similar preparation to the frog until it is normal again. More serious cases require veterinary attention.

Some lameness is due to self-inflicted injury, e.g., the pony striking one leg with another, and causing cuts and bruises, as in cases of brushing and overreach. This usually occurs because the pony is young, unfit, tired, or has faulty action. Such animals will require special protection for their legs.

Bandages and Boots

The bandages which are put on an animal for work are quite different from those used in the stable to give warmth. An exercise bandage is usually of some slightly elastic material. It must always have a layer of cotton sheeting or other suitable padding underneath it. This can be cut so that it covers the pony's leg from just below the knee, to just above the fetlock, and is wrapped around the leg so that it is flat and smooth. The bandaging is then started over the padding material at the upper edge, leaving about half an inch of padding showing above the bandage, and continuing downwards to firmly cover the lower edge of the padding. The bandage is taken up again so that the tapes or Velcro closure can be neatly tied on the outside of the pony's cannon bone. Bandages must not be put on, or tied, too tight.

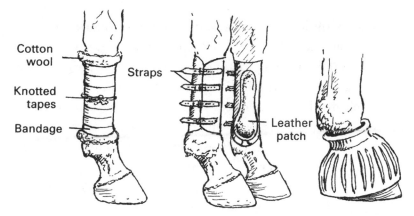

Cotton wool

Knotted tapes

Bandage

Straps

Leather patch

Fig. 62. Bandages and boots. Exercise bandage (left), boots (middle), and over-reach boot (right).

As an alternative to bandages, fitted boots are sometimes used to cover the cannon bone area. These are better for protection from knocks and bangs than they are for support. The boots are made of leather or fabric with leather reinforcement over vulnerable areas, such as the inside of the fetlock. Fastened with straps and buckles on the outside of the leg and with the straps pointing backwards, the boots need only be tightened enough to prevent them from slipping down. Care should be taken that grit does not get underneath them and rub the pony's skin.

Overreach boots are occasionally necessary, for some ponies' action is such that they cut the heels of their front feet with the inside rim of the toe of the back shoe. This is particularly likely to happen in very muddy, deep going. These overreach boots are made of rubber which will stretch sufficiently to go over the hoof, and the boot fits around the pastern to cover the endangered area.

Whether or not bandages and boots give worthwhile support to the leg is debatable, though they are often put on horses and ponies for this purpose. A wide variety of injuries to the bones and tendons of the leg, especially the lower leg, are possible, and a description of each one is really beyond the scope of this book.

Some of these injuries are more common than others, and some are also avoidable. Splints, for example, are bony lumps which develop on a pony's cannon bone. They only affect young animals, and are the result of working an immature pony whose bones are not fully developed. Repeated jarring causes minute fractures in the splint bones on the inside edge of the cannon, in the forelegs below the knee. These are painful and make the pony lame. Though large splints are unsightly, they seldom cause lameness once they have finished their own development. This problem can quite obviously be avoided by not riding young ponies for long periods, and on hard surfaces.

Laminitis is another type of lameness which is often avoidable. It differs from most other forms in that it affects all four limbs, though it is hard to miss, as it is excruciatingly painful. The laminae of all four feet became very hot, inflamed, and thickened. A pony with laminitis often lies down, is reluctant to move, or eat, and may look very much like a colic sufferer, although the burning heat of the feet will help to distinguish between the two conditions.

Prompt veterinary treatment is essential to reduce the permanent changes which result from laminitis as much as possible. These may make the pony unfit for anything but light work, if that. After laminitis the hoof becomes deformed, with a dropped (or convex) sole instead of the normal concave one, and the pony may take to standing noticeably on the heels. With modern treatment, an attack of laminitis may be quite brief, but it will still produce founder rings—ridges around the wall of the hoof which gradually grow out.

And the cause of laminitis? It is most common in overfed ponies, which are allowed to stuff themselves with grass when it is at its richest in the early summer. Though laminitis occurs occasionally in ponies which are already sick for some other reason, obesity is a far more common cause. Laminitis is one of the most common health problems in ponies, and one that can be prevented. To prevent laminitis, it is essential that a pony that tends to be overweight or has suffered from laminitis previously, should not have access to rich grazing in early summer (it may have to be stabled for this purpose) and should not be given more than the minimum amount of concentrates at any time of the year.

Chapter Fifteen

BUYING A PONY

You know you want a pony. You have decided that you can afford to keep one. The next problem is that of purchasing a suitable animal. Of course anyone can go out and buy a pony, but will it be the right pony for the purpose, and will it be a fair price? Horse dealing has the justifiable reputation of bringing out a dishonest streak in the most upstanding of people. Take care not to be misled into paying an exorbitant price for a totally unsuitable animal.

Another problem is the quantity of free advice which is offered by self-styled experts; much of this has to be taken with a large grain of salt. This does not mean that you should not accept advice from those more experienced than yourself; far from it, but it is wise to listen to several points of view.

Before embarking on a pony hunt, decide just what sort of pony is required. This depends greatly on the age and size of the person who is to ride it, since this will determine the approximate height of the animal that will be selected. A rough guide is that a pony up to 12.2 hh will carry someone twelve years old or less, one between 12.2 and 13.2 hh can accommodate a rider twelve to fourteen years old, and a pony 13.2 to 14.2 hh is suitable for a rider up to sixteen years of age; an animal over 14.2 hh (which is technically a horse) will probably be needed for someone bigger than this. For a young rider who is already big for his age, ponies bigger than the average size will be required, because it is better to buy a pony that is a little too large than to purchase one that is rather small, and will be rapidly outgrown.

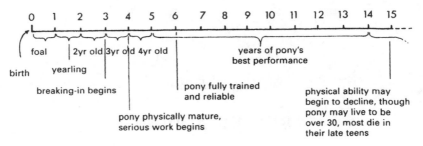

Fig. 63. A pony's life.

Consider also whether a mare or gelding is preferred. A mare can be kept for breeding when even the youngest member of the family has grown too big to ride her. Geldings, on the other hand, are said to be more reliable in temperament and performance.

A First Pony

After the height range, the next aspect to consider is the type of work for which the pony will be used. A first pony must above all be absolutely quiet and sweet tempered. Appearance is not of great importance. Neither is age, though the pony should be well beyond the difficult adolescent stage. A minimum of six or seven years old is best. Many a first pony can look back over twenty or more years of service to young riders. There is much to be said in favor of such a venerable animal in terms of sense and reliability. Slight physical deterioration due to age may be overlooked, though the vet's opinion should be the deciding factor in such matters.

It is important that a young rider is not frightened by his or her first pony. One of the most ridiculous situations which arises all too frequently is when the novice rider is given a young pony, sometimes no more than a six-month-old foal, 'so that they can grow up together.' Young ponies are strong, and require firm handling and training to make them safe and pleasant to ride. It is difficult to see how an inexperienced person, worse yet, a young child, can be expected to cope with such an animal.

Kind temperament is of paramount importance when dealing with a first pony. The next consideration is that of shape. Some ponies are rather broad through the barrel. This will overly stretch a small rider's short legs, and the saddle may slip around the plump middle. The pony must also be safe in traffic, even if it is unlikely to be ridden on the road except on a leading rein.

A Second Pony

A young rider builds up confidence with a first pony. Inevitably there comes a time when the animal becomes too small and has to be replaced. In a second pony, as with any other, good temperament, gentleness, and freedom from vice or bad behavior are essential. In this animal, however, absolute docility is not usually so important, and liveliness—so long as it does not amount to taking advantage of the rider—is generally an advantage. It makes the riding more fun, and usually means that the pony has greater capabilities as far as jumping, local shows, and other events are concerned.

Steadiness in traffic is of course vital in the second pony. This animal will probably be expected to carry a relatively inexperienced rider along public highways. The animal's age is important, too, since more strenuous work may be required. Young ponies should probably be avoided. Generally those between six and twelve years old are able to do all that is required of them, provided they are physically fit. Indeed, many older animals also perform well, and have the advantage of being less expensive than those in the prime of life.

Cost comes into the picture when deciding what sort of pony is wanted. The animal's age, appearance, breeding, and past performance all play a part in raising or lowering the price. Appearance and breeding are also significant in the cost of keeping the pony. A finely bred animal will be more expensive to feed and will probably need to be stabled. A sturdier type of pony will live happily in a field, with just a shelter and relatively little extra food.

Some ponies are offered for sale as specialists in certain types of work. If the animal has won a few show jumping competitions the price will increase accordingly. Some of these mounts may require very skilful handling and a competent or expert rider. It is easy to overestimate riding ability, and it is not really very wise to buy an animal which may frighten a rider who is unable to cope with it. More fun may be had from an ordinary pony that can in turn be a trail horse, a hunter, a show mount, a jumper, or even a driving pony.

Where to Look for the Pony

Have a rough picture in mind of the size and weight-carrying ability, hardiness and age, of the animal wanted, and probably the approximate price? Now where do you find a pony for sale? If there is a professional horse dealer in the area, he may be the best person to go to. This may seem surprising, but a well-established dealer has his reputation to consider, and is unlikely to sell a real dud to someone living locally. Nevertheless, when buying a pony, it is best for the buyer to beware. Guarantees and promises regarding the animal have to be treated warily, for there is seldom any recourse unless actual fraud can be proven, and this is rarely possible.

Novices often ask for trouble by going to a dealer and trying to pretend they are expert judges of horseflesh. To the professional it is of course obvious that they are not. Indeed, though the dealer might try to find an appropriate animal, the know-it-all may go so far as to sell himself a completely unsuitable horse but, in his wisdom, he is impossible to discourage.

If you know little about buying ponies, it is best to admit the fact. State what type of pony you want and for what purpose, and leave it to the dealer to find something to fit the bill. He will probably charge more than you might have paid elsewhere, but— provided he is reputable—you will have had the benefit of his experience in picking out a suitable pony. He will probably be willing to give you some help with your new acquisition as well.

The alternative is to buy a pony from a private home. Since animals are being outgrown by their young riders all the time, there is a constant stream of children's ponies for sale. It should not be forgotten, however, that some come on the market because they have been unsatisfactory in other ways. Do not make the error of believing that a private vendor is bound to be honest in dealings with ponies. There are a minority of pony enthusiasts who supplement their incomes by buying unlikely looking ponies, cleaning them up, and selling them on as "family pets—to good homes only." These animals can be good performers, though usually a pony that passes from hand to hand does so for a good reason, such as a vice, physical weakness, or poor performance.

Ponies are offered for sale in the advertisement columns of many local papers. A local riding club may also know of children's ponies for sale and, even better, may also know something about their temperament and performance records. It may take some time to find the right pony. It would be very foolish to rush into a purchase and be stuck with an animal that is unsuitable for the work required, and which may cause you problems when selling it later.

The worst instance of rushing blindly into the purchase of a pony is to buy one at a public auction. This is definitely a place

Fig. 64. Public auctions are for experts only.

for experts only. There is seldom an opportunity at a sale to give the animal a thorough trial and examination, or for the young rider to consider whether he really likes a pony. Although prices at auctions may be low compared with those of a good dealer or a private seller, buying at auction has often proven to be a poor choice.

Looking at the Pony

Going to look at a pony—potentially your own—is always exciting, but the prospective owner should not be carried away by the occasion and forget to give everything careful consideration. The pony has to be sized up carefully, because you must decide on the basis of your own and the vet's examination.

The pony's attitude when approached in the stable will tell you a lot. Is this visitor regarded with friendly interest? Do those gentle, large eyes have a kind expression? Some people scorn those who consider a pony's facial expression important, but the animal with the small, "piggy" eye, and a mean look is often ill-tempered. The pony should allow people to walk up to it, and should show no sign of viciousness or nervousness. If children are to be carried by it, the pony should not resent handling of the legs or ears, or picking up of the feet.

The pony's general appearance should be compact, with a shortish back, sloping hindquarters, and a neck which is neither long and "upside-down," so that it looks like a swan's, nor so short and thick that the pony will be able to pull like a train. A pretty head, with a flat or dished forehead, and fine features are desirable. General alertness suggests reasonable intelligence.

Shoulders should be sloping, with withers that carry the saddle well. Some ponies are so wide in the back that it is hard to find their withers at all; others are so bony and their withers so high that they are like riding on top of a fence; the happy medium is most desirable. Legs should be straight and strong, which is not the same as the thick heavy treetrunks of an under-size drafthorse. The feet should be round, with broad frogs and

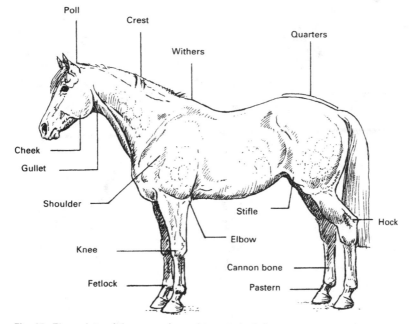

Fig. 65. The points of the pony. A good type to look for.

a wide open heel, not little, narrow boxes which are subject to damage by concussion.

If the overall appearance and demeanor of the pony is pleasant, then it should be seen ridden. Usually the seller provides a rider who will show off the animal's paces and jump it over a fence or two. It is smart not to be too impressed by this performance. Keep in mind that some of these young riders may be skilful at getting the best out of a pony, and the jumping of fences in the home paddock is frequently well-practiced. While the dealer's jockey is riding, note what bit and other tack is being used to control the pony, and, if possible, have it ridden on the road to see its reaction to traffic.

Next, the pony should be tried out by the individual who may be the animal's future rider. Gently walk the pony around the paddock for a few minutes, then try a steady trot in circles to the right and left. There should be no reluctance on the part of the pony to go either way. There should be no problems with cantering on either the right or left lead. Try to make your trial

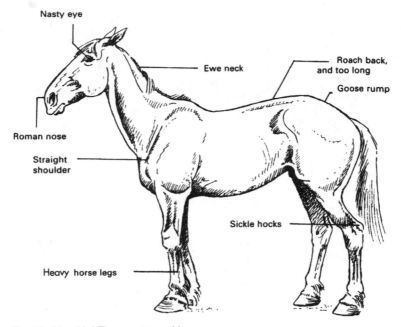

Fig. 66. Not this! The type to avoid.

ride different from the one given by the owner. Also try to include a specific test to check that the pony will stop obediently when heading for the stables, and that there is no reluctance to turn away from them. If the pony fails this test, it could be the first sign of a rebellious nature, which can be hard to cure. Finally, take the pony over a small fence.

In choosing a pony, it is important that the temperament should match that of the rider. A bold young person will enjoy riding a bold pony, while someone who is rather timid will do better on a more stoic animal. This does not mean that any pony should be unwilling to take a step unless it is beaten on. Such animals are tedious to ride, and encourage the rider to flap legs and arms like the sails of a windmill, in an attempt to make the pony move.

If you consider the pony to be suitable there are a few points which should be asked about. Is the pony easy to catch? Are there problems with tying, shoeing, or clipping? Does the animal walk readily into a trailer? The matter of breeding, if it is known, should be considered, and that of height, which can be important in children's ponies. For most competitive events, classes are divided on the basis of height, so that a pony of, say, 13.2 hh may be at a disadvantage in having to compete against some animals a few inches bigger.

The pony's diet should also be discussed. It is not unknown for someone to buy a quiet and well-schooled pony and take it home. Within a week the animal has become unmanageable from being fed an unaccustomed grain ration that is too rich.

Veterinary Examination

A final consideration is the question of whether the pony is physically fit and suitable for the work you want it to do. This is a matter for your own veterinarian, who examines the animal on your behalf, and at your expense.

You should, of course, tell your veterinarian just what purpose you are buying the pony for, whether it's to be as a general purpose child's pony, or as a show pony, for example. Some physical blemishes, such as scars or certain bony enlargements on a pony's

Fig. 67. Measuring a pony. The height is measured in hands (one hand equals four inches) and inches, and is taken from the highest point of the animal's withers. Half an inch is allowed for shoes.

legs, make no difference to a pony used for trail riding or small, local events. They could, however, seriously affect the chances of a show pony winning a championship event.

The term "sound" has been deliberately omitted. Though it is widely used by those associated with horses, its meaning is rather unclear. Generally a pony is considered sound if it is physically fit, and has had no past or present injuries which affect its capability to perform the work which might reasonably be expected of such an animal. The problem is that there are degrees of soundness. A horse that is expected to complete a very taxing combined-training three-day-event, or to jump seven feet or more, can have none of the slight signs of wear and tear that would be quite acceptable in a pony that will be asked to do no more than a day's hunting or a long trail ride now and then. This

Biting: Painful for the
victim.

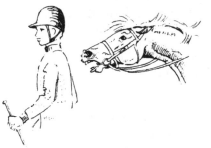

Bucking: The pony humps the back and tries to dislodge the rider.

Bolting: Galloping away ignoring the instructions of the rider.

Fig. 68. Equine vices to avoid. (i)

is taken into account during the vet's examination of the pony, for he could not, and would not, look for superlative physical fitness, nor would he find it in the majority of ponies.

The veterinarian nevertheless should make a thorough examination of a pony on behalf of a prospective purchaser. Any defects found, whether they will affect the pony's performance or not, will be noted, along with his opinion as to whether or not the pony is a good buy.

Cribbing: The pony gnaws at the manger, doors, fences etc.

Kicking people: The pony lashes out with the hind legs, usually unexpectedly.

Kicking the stable: With front or hind legs, sometimes just for impatience, sometimes apparently to inflict damage.

Balking: The pony would rather stay at home, or with other ponies, etc. Evidenced by refusing to go, or moving very slowly away from the stable, but will go as fast as possible towards it.

Fig. 69. Equine vices to avoid. (ii)

Rearing: Pony stands on hind legs; dangerous as the animal may over-balance and fall on top of rider.

Tearing clothing: A pony chews rug, etc. because of boredom, wrong feeding, dental troubles, being too hot, or just plain mischief.

Weaving: The pony stands at a door or gate, and sways from side to side, getting into a trance.

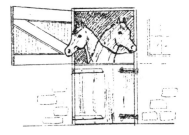

Wind-sucking: Arching the neck, the pony gulps down air.

Fig. 70. Equine vices to avoid. (iii)

If the pony is satisfactory in all respects, the final step is to pay, and arrange to get the animal home. Some dealers will deliver the pony, others will suggest the services of a professional transporter to deliver the animal. Either way, payment should be made when the pony comes into your care. Unfortunately, in most horse dealing one has no recourse if it is found, upon getting home, that the pony is not quite what it was thought to be. There is much to be said for asking the advice of an experienced horseman when going to look at a pony. This, combined with your own common sense and the vet's opinion, should help in the completion of a fair purchase.

Insurance

Buying a pony and its tack can represent a sizeable financial investment, and accidents and illness may mean extra unforeseen expenses. Though most first-time horse owners and those with strictly pleasure mounts would consider it an unnecessary expense, insurance is one thing to be considered after deciding to buy a new pony. The most important risk to be insured against is public liability. This covers the cost of damage to property or vehicles, or injury to other animals or people, caused by the pony getting loose, or kicking out. Many family household insurance policies include a public liability clause which covers a pony, and may also include theft of tack. It is worth checking the fine print on such a policy, or phoning the insurance company, and if this is not covered, taking out a separate policy. Ponies can also be insured against death, for loss of use, or for vets' fees. "Loss of use" insurance is very expensive, but can be worthwhile for show ponies, whose value can be greatly reduced through injury. A veterinary examination is usually required by the insurers before loss of use cover is accepted. Mortality and vet fees insurance are relatively inexpensive, and are a sensible way of budgeting for unforeseen disasters.

Glossary

Aged. The age of a pony can be told pretty accurately from his teeth until he is fifteen years old; any older than this, he is described as *aged*.

Arab. A breed of horses from North Africa. Lightly built and fast, strong and sound, with great intelligence and beauty. They have been crossbred with horses and ponies all over the world to introduce quality to native stock.

Backing can mean going backwards, but may also describe the process of getting on a young pony's back for the first time.

Bay is a particular color, and describes ponies with brown bodies and muzzles, and black manes, tails, and legs.

Bit and bitting. The *bit* is essentially a bar of metal held in the pony's mouth by the bridle used to guide and control the animal. *Bitting* is the training of a young pony to accept and respond to a bit.

Black. A pony is described as *black* only if he has a black muzzle as well as a black body, though he may have a few white markings.

Blaze. A broad white stripe down the front of a pony's face.

Breaking-in is training a pony to carry a rider (or draw a carriage) quietly and obediently. This term may be shortened to *breaking*, so an animal may be described as being *broken* or *unbroken*.

Breaking out can have its customary meaning of escaping from a field or stable, but in horsey terminology it also can means that an animal is beginning to sweat.

Broken knees are knees scarred where the pony has fallen and injured them.

Brown ponies are dark brown in color with brown muzzles, which distinguishes them from *black* ponies; and brown manes and tails, which distinguishes them from *bays*.

Brushing could indicate grooming, but also describes a fault in the pony's action where he hits one fore or hind leg with the other as he moves; it may also be described as *going close* in front or behind. Boots or bandages may be necessary to protect the animal's lower legs from injury.

Cannon bone. The straight bone which runs from the knee or hock to the fetlock.

Capped elbow results from repeated bruising of a pony's elbow which causes a large, soft, and ugly, though usually painless, swelling.

Capped hock describes a similar swelling on the hock.

Cast. While lying down, a pony may become trapped against a wall or fence so that he cannot get up; he is then described as *cast.* The word is used in a different context in *casting a shoe* (also called throwing a shoe), which means that the shoe has fallen off the pony's foot.

Chestnut ponies have reddish or golden colored bodies, manes, and tails, possibly with white markings. Ponies whose color is a bit darker (more or less that of cooked liver), are called *liver chestnut. Chestnuts* are also the normal horny excrescences on the insides of the pony's legs, above the knee, and below the hock.

Cob is a confusing term. To some people, it describes a size of animal approximately 13.2 to 15 hh. A *cob* may also be just a small and substantial animal, capable of carrying a heavy rider, and from this usage comes the term *cobby,* meaning an animal of small but sturdy build.

Colt. A young male pony which has not yet been castrated or used at stud, usually up to three years old; a *colt foal.*

Connemara. A breed of ponies native to Ireland and known for their tractability, soundness, and intelligence. They are good riding ponies between 13 and 14.2 hh and are most often gray or dun in color.

Corns are also the horny, bruised areas produced by shoes which are left on a pony's feet too long between shoeings.

Curb. A bit acting on the lever principle, tightening a *curb chain* around the pony's lower jaw. A *curb* is also a type of hock injury which animals with sickle-shaped, rather than normally angled, hocks are prone.

Dock. The part of a pony's tail composed of bone, muscle, and skin from which grow the long tail hairs. *Docking,* that is removing all or part of the dock, is no longer done, though it was somewhat common in the past, and is still sometimes done when a veterinarian finds that an injury to the tail makes it unavoidable.

Dorsal stripe. A black stripe running along the middle of a pony's back, often seen on dun or bay animals.

Dun indicates a honey-brown colored body with a black mane, tail, and often black legs as well. The name *dun* may also be given to a light brown pony, though that is less common.

Electric fence. Widely used by farmers, it consists of easily moved insulated sticks, or metal posts, standing about three feet high, and carrying a wire through which is passed a small, intermittent, electric current, generated by a battery unit that makes a loud ticking sound. After one shock, animals acquire great respect for this type of fence.

Feather is the long hair found on the back of the legs or the heels on some ponies.

Filly. A young female pony, who has not yet been bred; a *filly foal.*

Gelding. A male pony that has been castrated.

Gestation. The period between a mare's being bred to a stallion, or covered, and giving birth to her foal; the average gestation period is 336 to 340 days, though considerable variation is normal.

Girth. The broad strap buckled around a pony to hold the saddle in place.

Gray. Equines are usually described as *gray* rather than white, possibly because ponies are rarely truly white, because of extraneous dark hairs mixed in the coat. A *flea-bitten gray* has speckles of gray and brown all over the body, while a *dappled gray* has a steely gray colored coat, matted with lighter and darker areas.

Hacking is casual riding along roads, trails, and bridlepaths, either for pleasure, or to get to a particular location.

Hands. A pony is measured in *hands*, one hand measured as four inches, and height is described as, for example, thirteen *hands* three inches, or 13.3 hh (the hh standing for *hands high*).

Horse. This can simply mean any equine of 14.2 hh or more, or it may sometimes be used to describe a stallion rather than a gelding or mare.

Loins. The part of the pony's back between saddle and rump, it is weaker and more sensitive than other areas of the body.

Longeing. Exercising or training a pony by making him trot, on a long, or *longeing*, rein, in circles around the trainer. Also spelled *lungeing*.

Mare. A female pony over the age of three years.

Markings on ponies are usually white, and are found mainly on the face and legs; their individual shapes and sizes can be useful for describing and identifying a pony.

Martingale. A piece of equipment used to keep a pony's head or reins in the correct position.

Mouth. The pony eats just as any other animal does, but the mouth also carries the bit, and the animal's responsiveness to the rider's signals depends on its sensitivity. A *good mouth* or a *light mouth* is very sensitive, while a *hard mouth* has been injured by rough handling and has little feeling for the bit and the rider's hands.

Nappy ponies are rebellious and resent leaving their fields or stables, walking slowly, stopping, refusing to go on, etc., on the outward journey, but traveling as fast as they are allowed when turned for home.

Palomino ponies are a golden color with white manes and tails.

Pinto is a mixed color, exhibiting large random patches of a darker color, interspersed with white. The mane and tail may be all black or all white or multi-colored.

Pitchfork. A long-handled fork with two or more slender, sharp prongs, used for moving hay and straw and cleaning the stall.

Pony. Usually equines of 14.2 hh and under are called *ponies*, though animals used for playing polo, regardless of their size, are also called *ponies*.

Prick. An injury caused by a nail, or similar sharp object, being driven through the horn of a pony's hoof, and into the sensitive part of the foot.

Roan ponies have coats which are an even mixture of white interspersed with some other color. A *blue roan* is black or dark brown plus white, giving a slightly blue appearance; a *red roan* is bay or bay-brown mixed with white; and a *strawberry roan* is chestnut mixed with white hairs.

Saddlery sizes. Saddlery is sold in different sizes. *Pony size* will usually fit animals up to about 13.2 hh or so. *Full size* is for animals standing 15 hh and above. Saddles are measured in inches from front (pommel) to back (cantle) and are also designated *narrow, medium,* or *broad* according to the width of the back of the animal they are intended to fit.

Schooling. Riding a pony in order to train it, in a marked arena, or *school* in the field.

Shetland. The smallest of Britain's native breeds, the *Shetland* (whose size is usually stated in inches) is often under 40 inches tall. Small and tough, it has great strength of both body and mind.

Snaffle. A type of bit consisting of a straight or jointed bar. Contact with the rider's hands, through the reins, is direct rather than through a lever system, as it is in the curb bit.

Snip. A small white marking in the region of the pony's nostrils.

Socks. A white marking on the leg(s) no higher than the fetlock.

Stallion. An uncastrated male pony, usually one used at stud.

Star. Any white marking on a pony's forehead may be called a *star.*

Stripe generally means a narrow white stripe down a pony's face.

Stocking is the term used to describe a white marking on the leg(s) running up to the knee or hock.

Tack. Both bridle and saddle, as well as other pieces of horse equipment, are referred to as tack; saddling the pony may be called *tacking up.*

Thoroughbred, sometimes abbreviated as *TB.* The Thoroughbred is an English breed which has evolved through centuries of crossing imported, mainly Arab, stock with native British breeds to produce the fast, athletic, beautiful and sometimes highly strung animals seen on modern racecourses. The Thoroughbred has been used to introduce some of its size and *quality,* that is, its lightness of body, and its speed to the progeny of Thoroughbred–pony crosses.

Vice. A bad habit acquired by a pony, such as persistent kicking in the stable, or biting. A *vicious pony* is one which has a vice involving deliberately injuring humans or other animals, such as lashing out at them with the hind feet, or chasing people in the field.

Wall eye. An eye which is pink or blue, rather than the more normal dark brown color.

Welsh ponies are indigenous to the British Isles, and the breed is noted for its attractive appearance and pleasant temperament. Welsh ponies are excellent for riding, with the most common colors gray, dun, cream and chestnut. *Welsh cobs,* which are derived from the Welsh Mountain pony, are larger animals, up to 15.2 hh, and strong, with fine knee action at the trot. This breed is popular for both driving and riding.

Index

A

Accommodations, 27–34
Acres of grazing per pony, 17
Acute hearing, 6
Age, 3
Aged
  definition, 179
Alertness, 6
Alfalfa cubes, 72
Allergy-triggering dust particles,
  140
Animal's droppings, 58
Anthelmintics, 133
Anti-allergy nebulization, 141
Appetite, 44
Apples, 74
Approaching, 7
Arab, 144
  crossbred ponies, 144
  definition, 179
Area per pony, 60–61
Asthmatic attacks, 140
Attitude, 170
Automatic water dish, 46
Azoturia, 143

B

Backing
  definition, 179
Balking
  illustrated, 175
Bandages, 97–98, 131
  for protection
    illustrated, 98
  reasons for, 97–98
  for warmth
    illustrated, 98
  for work, 160–163

Barley straw, 37
Barn, 9
Basics, 3
Basic shelter, 10
Bay
  definition, 179
Bed, 35–44
  making, 40–41
Bedding, 30
  eating, 43–44
  material
    types of, 37–38
Beet sugar, 72
Behavior
  corrected immediately, 6
  rewards for, 8
Benefits, 1–2
Binocular vision, 5
Bit
  definition, 179
  proper fitting, 105
  types
    illustrated, 106
    material for, 105
Biting, 174
Bit ring
  illustrated, 103
Bitting
  definition, 179
Black
  definition, 179
Blanket, 12. *See also* Rugs
  care, 13
  clip, 93
    illustrated, 90
  heavy
    illustrated, 95
  need or not, 94–95

Blanket, *(continued)*
 proper fit
  illustrated, 93
 put on, 94
 types of, 94
 wearing, 13
Blaze
 definition, 179
Blunt spikes, 106
Board, 9
Boarding locations, 17
Body brush, 77
 illustrated, 76
Bolting, 174
Boots
 knee, 98–99
 knee-high riding, 120
 for work, 160–163
Boredom, 44
Box stall
 illustrated, 28
Bradoon, 106
 illustrated, 109
Braiding
 mane, 83
  illustrated, 84
Bran, 73–74
Bran mash, 73–74
Breaking-in
 definition, 179
Breaking out
 definition, 179
Breeding, 172
 period, 146
Bridle, 104–108
 elements, 104
 illustrated, 103
Bridling, 110–111
 illustrated, 110
Broken knees
 definition, 179
Browband, 104
 illustrated, 103

Brown
 definition, 179
Brushing
 definition, 179–180
 winter procedure, 89
Buckets, 25
Buckling, 174
Bulbs of heels
 illustrated, 150
Buying, 2. *See also* Purchasing

C
Cannon bone
 definition, 180
 illustrated, 153
Cantle
 illustrated, 113
Capped elbow
 definition, 180
Capped hock
 definition, 180
Carrots, 74
Cast
 definition, 180
Castration, 146
Catches, 32
Catching, 61–62
Cavesson noseband
 illustrated, 109
Central cleft of frog
 illustrated, 150
Cheek, 106
 illustrated, 107
Cheekpiece
 illustrated, 103, 104
Chestnut
 definition, 180
 function, 87–88
Chronic obstructive pulmonary
  disease (COPD), 140
Clean fresh water, 24
Cleaning
 stable, 38–39

equipment for, 42
water bucket, 45–46
Clenches, 154
Clip
  how to, 91–92
Clipping, 89–101
  styles, 92–93
  illustrated, 90
Clothing, 89–101
  how much, 95
Coat, 129
  condition for clipping, 91
Cob
  definition, 180
Colds, 139–142
Colic, 26, 135–139
  cause, 135–136
  illustrated, 136
  what to do, 138
Colt
  definition, 180
Comb. *See also* Brushing
  curry, 77
  illustrated, 76
Compacted clay
  flooring, 37
Companionship, 23–24
Concentrate feeds, 50
Concrete floor, 36
Condition
  feed according to, 67–69
Connemara
  definition, 180
Consistent, 6
Cooler, 96–97
Corns
  definition, 180
Coronary band
  illustrated, 149
Correcting, 6
Corrugated iron, 30
Cost, 167. *See also* Purchasing
  of purchasing, 3

Coughs, 139–142
  cause, 140
Covered, 146
Cracked or greasy heels, 81
Cribbing
  illustrated, 175
Curb
  definition, 180–181
Curb bit, 106
Curb chain, 108
  illustrated, 107
Curb chain hook
  illustrated, 107
Curb rein, 107, 108
Curb ring
  illustrated, 107
Curry comb, 77

D
Daily exercise, 11, 122
Dandy brush, 77
  illustrated, 76
Deep litter system, 42–43
Demeanor, 171
Dentist, 134–135
Digital cushion, 151
Distension
  of intestine, 137
Dock
  definition, 181
Door, 31–33
  catches, 32
Doorways, 31–33
  size, 31
Dorsal stripe
  definition, 181
Do's and don'ts, 3
Double bridle, 106
  illustrated, 109
Dry stone walls, 18
Dry vermin-proof container,
  50
D-shaped ring, 108

Dun
  definition, 181

E
Eating
  bedding, 43–44
  habits, 68
  suggestions, 69
Education, 1
Eggbutt snaffle, 106
Electrical installation, 34
Electric clippers, 91
Electric fence, 19–20
  definition, 181
Energy
  feed according to, 67–69
Equipment
  grooming, 75–79
Ergot, 87
Event
  day after, 128
  day before, 123–124
  over, 127–128
  pony's welfare, 126
Exercise, 11, 119
  feed according to, 66–67
  program, 145
Exercise bandage
  illustrated, 161
Exertional rhabdomyolysis,
    143–145
Eyesight, 5, 6, 129
  discharge, 130

F
Facial expression, 170
Fall. *See* Seasons
Family member
  pony, 1–8
Farrier's work, 154
Feather
  definition, 181
Feces
  impaction, 138

Feed bucket
  per pony, 69
Feeding, 3
  concentrate, 50
  extra, 65–74
  hay, 48
  pelleted products, 72–77
  proper storage, 49
  quality, 66
  routine, 70–71
  suggestions, 69
  times
    all at same time, 69
    winter, 12
Feet, 149–163
  appearance, 170
  bones
    illustrated, 153
  cleaning, 79
  picking up
    illustrated, 152
  scraping
    rats' tails, 79–80
Felt bandages, 131
Female foal, 146, 181
Fences, 17–20
  electric, 19–20
  ideal type, 18
  mending, 4
  types, 18
Fertilizer
  illustrated, 40
Fetlock joint
  illustrated, 153
Fetlocks
  removed, 87
  trimmed, 87
Fields, 3, 9–15, 17–26
  dangers, 22–23
  foraging for food, 17
  overgrazed, 58–60
  pony-proof, 17
  rented, 17
  shelters, 27

Filly, 146
    definition, 181
Fire, 53–54
Fire extinguisher, 54
First pony, 166–167
Flies, 10
Flooring, 35–44
    compacted clay, 37
    type, 36–37
Foaling, 146
Food. *See* Feeding
Foot. *See* Feet
Footgear, 120
Foreleg lameness, 158
Frightened pony, 5
Frog, 151
    illustrated, 150
Frost nails, 156
Full-cheek snaffle, 106
Fully clipped out
    illustrated, 90
Fulmer snaffle, 106

G
Gallop, 70
Garden fertilizer
    illustrated, 40
Gates, 30
Gateways, 20–21
Gelding, 147
    definition, 181
Gestation
    definition, 181
    period, 146
Get out, 22
Girth, 114
    cleaning, 117
    definition, 181
    illustrated, 113
Grass, 11
    and hay, 62–64
    as pony food, 55–64
    summer *vs.* winter, 55
Grass-fed only method, 15

Grassland
    damage, 17
Gray
    definition, 181
Grazing, 9, 55–57, 70
    acreage needed per pony, 17
Grooming, 75–88
    equipment, 75–79
        box, 76
        illustrated, 76
    kit, 79
    outdoor pony, 79–80
    tails, 79–80
    tray, 79
    winter coat, 89
Group rides, 119
Gullet
    illustrated, 113

H
Hacking, 119
    definition, 182
Hair, 129
Half-acre paddock, 9
Half-and-half turnout system, 12–14
Half-moon snaffle, 106
Halters, 51–52
    illustrated, 51
Handling, 3
    head, 8
Hands
    definition, 182
    measuring
        illustrated, 173
Hard hat, 120
Hay
    amount, 63
        winter and summer, 64
    and grass, 62–64
    quality of, 62–64
Hay net, 48
    for event, 127
    illustrated, 49
    per pony, 69

Hayrack, 48
Head guards, 100
Headpiece, 104
  buckles, 104
Healthy, 17
  identification signs, 129
Heavy blanket
  illustrated, 95
Heel
  illustrated, 149
Height, 173
Herbivorous animals, 5
Hind leg lameness, 159
Hinges, 31
Hock boots, 98–99
  illustrated, 99
Hogging, 82
Home
  for pony, 9–15
Hoof, 150–153
  illustrated, 149
  underside of
    illustrated, 150
Hoof oil and brush
  illustrated, 76
Hoof pick, 75
  illustrated, 76
Hooves, 129
Horse
  definition, 182
Horse-sick, 59
Housing, 27–34. *See also* Stable
Hunter clip, 92
  illustrated, 90
Hunter trials
  preparation, 123–124
Hunts, 2
  preparation, 123–124

I
Impaction colic
  reasons, 138
Influenza, 139
Insecticidal drugs, 142

Insurance, 177
Inter-pony relationships,
  23–24

J
Jodhpur boots, 120
Jointed snaffle, 105
  illustrated, 109
Jointed snaffle family, 106
Jumpers, 22

K
Keeper, 106
Kick catch, 32
Kicking
  belly, 136
  illustrated, 175
  people, 175
Kimberwicke, 108
  illustrated, 108
Knee boots, 98–99
  illustrated, 99
Knee-high riding boots, 120

L
Lameness, 122, 149,
  158–160
  caused by, 160
  illustrated, 159
Laminitis, 162–163
  cause, 162
  prevention, 163
Land. *See also* Fields
  rented, 17
Lead rope
  illustrated, 51
Leather
  cleaning, 117
Legs, 149–163
  bandages, 97–98
    illustrated, 95
  stable, 80
Lice, 142

Life span, 166
Light bulbs, 33–34
Lighting, 33–34
Lip strap
    illustrated, 107
Loading
    problems, 125
Lockjaw, 132
Loins
    definition, 182
Longeing
    definition, 182
Loose animals, 22
Lungeing
    definition, 182
Lying down, 11

M
Maintenance cost, 3
Mane, 81–83
    braiding, 83
        illustrated, 84
    direction, 81–82
    length, 82
    thickness, 82
Mane comb
    illustrated, 76
Mangers, 46–47
Manure
    disposal of, 39–40
    pile
        illustrated, 40
    stack
        illustrated, 40
Mare
    breeding age, 146
    definition, 182
Markings
    definition, 182
Martingales, 111–112
    definition, 182
Mated, 146
Measuring
    illustrated, 173

Medicines
    given by, 74
Medium-quality pasture, 57
Memory, 6
Mending
    fences, 4
Mild lameness, 158
Mind
    of pony, 4–7
Monday-morning disease,
        143–145, 145
Mouth
    definition, 182
Mucked out, 38

N
Nappy
    definition, 182
Navicular bone
    illustrated, 153
Nebulization, 140
Neckstraps, 111–112
Nervousness
    sign of, 170
New Zealand rug, 13, 96
    illustrated, 96
Night riding, 121
Nose
    discharge, 130
Nosebands, 108–109

O
Oats, 71
Oat straw, 37
Ordinary work, 119
Organized hunts
    preparation, 123–124
Outings, 119–128
Overgrazed pasture, 58–60
Overreach boots, 161

P
Paddock, 9–15, 17, 57–58. *See also*
        Fields

Pain
  signs of, 136
Palomino
  definition, 182
Parasites
  life cycle, 59
Parasitic worms, 132–134
Partial clip, 92
Partitions, 30
Pastern
  illustrated, 149
Pastern bone
  illustrated, 153
Pasture. *See also* Fields
  medium-quality, 57
  overgrazed, 58–60
Paving material, 36
Pawing ground, 137
Pedal bone
  illustrated, 153
Pelham
  bit, 108
  illustrated, 107
Pelleted feeds, 72–77
Physical blemishes, 173
Physically fit, 173
Picking
  pony's feet, 75
Pinto
  definition, 182
Pitchfork
  definition, 182
Plain curb bit
  illustrated, 109
Plastic curry comb
  illustrated, 76
Pleasure, 1
Points
  avoidance
    illustrated, 171
  to look for
    illustrated, 171
Poisonous shrubs, 57
Poisonous weeds, 57

Polish
  for coat, 80
Pommel
  illustrated, 113
Pony
  definition, 183
  family member, 1–8
Port, 107
Predatory beasts, 4–5
Prick
  definition, 183
Professional transporter,
    125
Public auctions, 169
Purchasing, 165–177
  cost of, 3
  what to look at, 170–173
  where to look, 168–170

Q
Quartering, 80–81
  illustrated, 149
Quarters
  for pony, 9–15

R
Rails, 30
Rearing
  illustrated, 176
Reins
  illustrated, 103
  material for, 105
Rented land, 17. *See also*
    Fields
Respiratory infection, 141
Rest, 139
Rewards, 8
Rhinoviruses, 139
Rider
  matched with pony, 165
  size and age, 165
  skill level
    learning, 3
  speed, 124–126

Riding boots
  knee high, 98–99, 120
Riding club, 169
Ringworm, 143
Road signs
  importance of, 120
Roan
  definition, 183
Roofs, 28–31
  types, 30
Roughage, 65
Rugs, 93. *See also* Blanket
  New Zealand
    illustrated, 96
    waterproof, 13

S
Saddle, 114–115
  illustrated, 113
Saddle flap
  illustrated, 113
Saddle pad
  illustrated, 113
Saddlery, 4
Saddlery sizes
  definition, 183
Saddle sores, 143
Saddling up, 116
  illustrated, 115
Salt licks, 47–48
Salt water, 130
Sawdust, 38
Schooling, 119
  definition, 183
Screed concrete surface, 36
Seasons, 9–10
  amount of hay, 63–64
  area per pony, 60–61
  care, 12–14
  coat, 89–101
  event, 128
  feed, 12
  feed according to, 67–69
  washing, 81

Seat
  illustrated, 113
Seat of corn
  illustrated, 150
Second pony, 167–168
Selection, 147
Sesamoid bone
  illustrated, 153
Sex life, 145–147
Shedding, 89–101
Shelter, 3, 9, 10
  building, 29
Shelter bedded down,
  11
Shelters
  field, 27
Shetland
  definition, 183
Shoe
  illustrated, 155
Shoeing, 3, 153–154
  against, 157–158
Shoulders
  appearance, 170
Shows, 2, 119
  preparation, 123–124
Shredded paper, 38
Shrubs
  poisonous, 57
Skill level
  riding
    learning, 3
Skin disease, 142–145
Skins, 7
Sleeping position, 11
Slip-rails, 21
Small trace clip
  illustrated, 90
Snaffle
  definition, 183
Snaffle rein, 107
Snaffle ring
  illustrated, 107
Sneezes, 139–142

Snip
  definition, 183
Socks
  definition, 183
Sole
  illustrated, 150
Special occasions, 123–128
Special outings, 119
Sponge, 78
  illustrated, 76
Spring. *See* Seasons
Stable, 11, 27–34
  bandages, 97–98
  building, 29
  cleaning, 38–39
    equipment, 42
  equipping, 45–54
  outside surroundings, 53
  requirements, 13
  size, 27
  types, 28–29
  water container, 45
Stabled pony, 14
Stable rubber, 78
Stabling ponies
  pros and cons, 15
Stall. *See also* Stable
  size, 27
Stallions, 146
  definition, 183
Stamping belly, 136
Standing martingales, 111
  illustrated, 112
Star
  definition, 183
Status symbol, 2
Stirrup leathers
  cleaning, 118
  examine, 118
Stirrup lights, 121
Stocking
  definition, 183
Stomach, 135–139

Storage area
  food, 49–50
  tack, 117
Straight snaffle, 106
Strangles, 141–142
  illustrated, 141
Straw, 37
Straw bales, 29
Stripe
  definition, 183
Stud farm, 146
Stud fee, 146
Sugar byproducts, 72
Sugar lumps, 8
Summer. *See also* Seasons
  amount of hay, 64
  area per pony, 60–61
  coat, 89–101
  washing, 81
Summer sheet, 97
Supervision, 4
Surgical colic, 137
Survive, 10
Sweat scraper, 78, 80
  illustrated, 76
Sweet itch, 142

T
Tack, 103–118
  cleaning, 116–118
  definition, 183
  storage, 117
Tail, 83–87
  illustrated, 86
Tail bandage, 85–86
  illustrated, 85
Tail guards, 100
Tapeworms, 133–134
Tearing clothing
  illustrated, 176
Teeth, 68
  illustrated, 135
Temperament, 172

Tetanus, 132
Tethering ring, 51
Thoroughbred
  definition, 184
Throat latch
  illustrated, 103
Toe
  illustrated, 149
Toe clip
  illustrated, 155
Tooth trouble, 134–135
Trace clip, 92
  illustrated, 90
Trail rides, 2
Traits
  avoidance
    illustrated, 171
  to look for
    illustrated, 171
Traveling
  boots, 101
  by horse trailer, 124–125
  ready for
    illustrated, 101
Treats, 8
Trimming, 87–88
Trough
  types, 24–25
Tucked up, 68
Tush
  illustrated, 135
Tying up, 52
  diease, 143–145, 144
  illustrated, 50–53

U
Unwell pony
  identification signs, 130
Uprooted weeds, 58

V
Vaccination, 139
  upon birth, 146

Ventilation, 31, 33–34
Verbal commands
  taught, 5–6
Veterinary care, 129–146
  required
    signs for, 131
Veterinary examination, 173
Vetrap, 98
Vice
  to avoid
    illustrated, 174, 175, 176
  definition, 184
Viciousness, 184
  sign of, 170
Viral disease
  prevention of, 139

W
Wall eye
  definition, 184
Walls, 28–31
  illustrated, 149
Wardrobe, 93–101
Warts, 142
Washing, 80–81
Water, 24
  for event, 127
  before feed, 69
  gallons per day
    per pony, 25
Water brush, 78
  illustrated, 76
Water bucket
  cleaning, 45–46
Water container
  stable, 45
Water dish
  automatic, 46
Waterproof New Zealand rug, 13
Weather, 9–10
  bad, 128
Weaving
  illustrated, 176

Weeds
 poisonous, 57
 uprooted, 58
Weight, 130
 feed according to, 67–69
Welsh ponies
 definition, 184
Wheat straw, 37
Whiskers, 87
Wild ponies, 4
Windows, 33–34
 types, 33
Wind sucking
 illustrated, 176
Winter. *See also* Seasons
 amount of hay, 63–64
 area per pony, 60–61
 coat, 89–101
 event, 128

feed, 12
 washing, 81
Wire getaways, 21
Wiring, 33–34
Wood shaving, 38
Work before food, 70
Worming, 132–134
 upon birth, 146
Worms, 58
 egg source, 59
 parasitic, 132–134
 ringworm, 143
 tapeworms, 133–134
Wound
 irrigation solutions, 131
 treatment, 130–132

Y
Yew, 57